Items should be returned on or before the last date shown below. Items not already requested by other borrowers may be renewed in person, in writing or by telephone. To renew, please quote the number on the barcode label. To renew online a PIN is required. This can be requested at your local library.
Renew online @ www.dublir
Fines charged for overdue ite
incurred in recovery. Damage
be charged to the borrower.

Leabharlanna Poiblí Chat
Dublin City Public Libraries

Baile Átha Cliath
Dublin City

Terenure Branch Tel: 4907035

Date Due	Date Due	Date Due
- 7 MAY 2016	28th June	
- 9 MAY 2016	3rd Aug 2016	
24th Aug 2016	6th Oct	

D0833979

HELP!
I'M TURNING
INTO MY
DAD!

**A GUIDE TO SURVIVING
YOUR MID-LIFE CRISIS**

THIS IS A PRION BOOK

This edition published in 2015 by Prion Books
An imprint of the Carlton Publishing Group
20 Mortimer Street
London W1T 3JW

First published in 2008
Reprinted in 2011

A CIP catalogue record for this book is available from the
British Library

ISBN: 978-1-85375-927-7

Printed in Dubai

10 9 8 7 6 5 4 3 2 1

HELP!
I'M TURNING
INTO MY
DAD!

A GUIDE TO SURVIVING
YOUR MID-LIFE CRISIS

PRION

To my Mum, my brother and – natch – my Dad.

Contents

Introduction   7

Chapter 1 – Dad Rock!   11
Chapter 2 – DIY Till I Die!   27
Chapter 3 – The Fairer Sex   43
Chapter 4 – Dadicated Follower Of Fashion!   55
Chapter 5 – One Man And His Dog   71
Chapter 6 – Booze!   85
Chapter 7 – May The Best Team Win!   101
Chapter 8 – Look After The Pennies   115
Chapter 9 – Send Us A Postcard   135
Chapter 10 – No Circulars!   145
Chapter 11 – You'll Get Square Eyes!   155

Appendix: Dad's Saturday Diary   171
Quiz: Are You Turning Into Your Dad?   177
Glossary: Talking A Good Game   183

Introduction

Are you becoming obsessed with DIY? Have you taken to packing a fold-up plastic mac before setting out on a day trip? Do you now regularly bark: "HOW much?" as you stomp around shops? Have you replaced binges with barbecues, gigs with gardening and Ibiza with the Isle of Wight? Are you suddenly unable to get up from a chair without emitting a weary groan?

In short, are you – gulp! – turning into your Dad? Rather looks like it, doesn't it?

Stop worrying, you're in good company and help is at hand! In the pages that follow, you'll find everything you need to help ease you into the anxious period of a man's existence when he looks in life's mirror and sees his father staring back at him. We're all in it together and everything is going to be fine. So just relax.

However much we swear it won't happen to us, all men reach that day when we realize, to our considerable horror, that we are starting to do and say all the things our father did. Behind the wheel of the car, down the pub of a Sunday lunchtime, watching football on TV, we are becoming well and truly set in his ways. It's as terrifying as it is inevitable and it's happening to you right now. Don't worry about denying it, we're all friends here and honesty is the name of the game.

Everywhere you look, you can watch men turning into their Dads. It's like a remake of the film The Bodysnatchers, but with even worse clothes and with receding hair. You see them wherever you go. There they are, previously frisky, happy-go-lucky men becoming increasingly grouchy and forgetful. Where they once strutted down the street with music blasting through headphones into their ears and a true sense of both swagger and direction, they now meander along, whistling away to themselves, looking lost and a bit befuddled. Sometimes, they even clean forget where it is they were going. If you try and strike up a conversation with them they will keep forgetting what your name is, and – in some cases – what their own name is.

Sounds harrowing, doesn't it? So what do these decaying dudes do to relax? It used to take them 10 minutes to arrange a night out with mates, now they spend up to 10 weeks arranging a get-together and the moment they arrive at any social function, they start letting it be known that they can't stay long. After all, they've got to be up early in the morning to fix that squeaking door upstairs, and in any case, they have found their stamina has deserted them when it come to socializing, and, well, more or less everything else.

You can also see them on the roads, playing their soft-rock compilations albums, as they drive to their local DIY megastore for an afternoon's indignant chorus of "HOW much?" There they are too, at football matches, uttering such ghastly phrases as "May the best team win", rather than cheering their team on as if their lives depended on it. From buying corduroys to checking their bank statements against the stubs in their chequebooks; from looking forward to the weather forecast at the end of the news to joining their local Neighbourhood Watch group, men everywhere are turning into their Dads.

So slip on your slippers, get your pipe out, put your feet up and enjoy this chastening account of inappropriate clothing, antiquated hairstyles, sensible drinking and cringesome catchphrases. You might even like to have a glass of port by your side as you flick through the pages to come. If you are on nodding terms with the staff of your nearest DIY megastore, if you've joined the local Neighbourhood Watch group and if you've decided that open-air picnic concerts are just simply more sensible than sweaty mosh-pit gigs, then you'll recognize and enjoy what you find.

Chapter 1

Dad Rock!

As you turn into your Dad, what will be the soundtrack of your life? Music is an appropriate place to begin our examination of those destined for Dad-dom because it is here more than anywhere that the evidence is clearest, and the decline most sharp and spectacular.

It's when you walk through the doors of a music store that you quickly discover whether or not you are turning into your Dad. Do you spend hour after hour, flicking through the shelves, in search of the latest CD by the latest achingly hip American artist? Do you spend half your wage packet on CDs of bands you haven't even heard of just because you think their name sounds cool? No?

Well, do you relish every moment of your time in the store, happy to spend time on the whole selection process? Are you likely to return to the store the following weekend to repeat the experience? No, I didn't think so. Because we all know that you simply head straight to the chart section, pick up a compilation of soft-rock driving music, pay for it at the counter and leave the store, saying to yourself: "That'll do me for another year."

A man loves his music but as he grows older and turns into his Dad, his relationship with music changes profoundly. Where he was once Born To Run, he now wonders if he was actually Born To Waddle. And when you find that you are spending more time using your lawn strimmer than listening to Joe Strummer you know you are most of the way to becoming your Dad. And as for Teenage Kicks, well all that seems an age ago to you now. Probably because it is, my friend.

Which is why your visits to record stores are now such rare and fleeting affairs. You're in and out in no time at all. You spend more time on the toilet. After all, how long do you need to spend in your local HMV if you know that you're going to buy the *Top Gear – Seriously Cool Driving Music* album? Complete with Paul McCartney's *Live And Let Die*, Whitesnake's *Is This Love* and Phil Collins *In The Air Tonight*, it is the soundtrack not just to your driving, but also to your increasingly Dad-like life! So slap it in the CD player, don your air guitar and let's rock!

However, go easy on the air guitar because, as the album's title neatly suggests, the *Top Gear* compilation is designed for listening to in your car. Have you found yourself looking for excuses to drive down the motorway, just so you can "burn rubber" to the strains of Whitesnake, Meatloaf, Macca et al? Come on, admit it, you have. It's better to be honest about it. "Like A Bat Outta Hell" you scream as your car passes 70 miles an hour. That's what you scream out loud, at any rate. Inside your head you are saying "Me? Old? I don't think so!" Which is deliciously ironic because every time you feel the need to sing along to Meatloaf in your car you are not confounding your increasingly old age, you are in fact confirming it!

WHAT DID YOU SAY YOUR NAME WAS?

As for what is in the charts at the moment, well you haven't got a clue any more, have you? It was the ghastly-but-hilarious racing pundit John McCririck who said: "I know nothing about music. I don't the difference between Mary J Bilge and Dildo." However, you don't even know that much, do you? As far as you are concerned, Amy Winehouse is the name of a vineyard, Joss Stone is the name of the latest range of Lynx deodorant and Lily Allen is a Chinese restaurant. You're unrepentant about this. The charts are rubbish anyway, kids nowadays' etc...

However, when it comes to live music, you're not quite ready to give that baby up yet. Not you, the veteran of numerous legendary rock concerts. There's nothing like live music to really enliven the soul. The communal feeling of the audience, the energy and excitement generated by the band, the leaping round at the front, shouting every single line along with the vocalist, the screaming them back on for an encore – "Come back and play some more music!" – it's all great fun... up to a certain age. Then, the day comes when suddenly your performance paradigm shifts and the whole concert experience becomes as tempting as the thought of naked group sex at an old people's home. And even more tiring. The audience becomes "a crowd" and you find that nowadays you don't like crowds; the energy and excitement of the band becomes exhausting, the shouting along with the band hurts your throat – plus you find you can't remember lyrics so well anymore – and as for the jumping around, well don't even go there unless you want to seriously put your back out. The encore seems a waste of time, too, as you will have left by then in order to catch the last train home. Well, it's just more sensible, isn't it?

Help is at hand, though. Just because these sorts of gigs

are no longer an option for you, that doesn't mean you have to retire from the whole live music arena all together. So as you emerge, sweaty, beery and exhausted from your next indoor gig, take a look back at the venue you've just left because it may well be the last time you see it. Spend some time reliving all those memories of gigs down the years: the mosh-pits, the arms in the air, the predictable encores and the "surprise" special guests. Wave them all goodbye and shut the door on that part of your life for good. You're done with the whole concert hall gig experience. It was fine while it lasted but it's time you moved on. However, just as men take a new woman "on the rebound" after a break-up, so you will need a new partner, having split up from the indoor gig experience.

Well, the new babe is right in front of you. From now on it will be the open-air concerts all the way for you. These events, staged at stately homes across the country, are the live music of choice for the man who is turning into his Dad. There you can turn up and listen to the warblings of easy listening artists. It's all far more suitable for you. Joss Stone, Will Young, Katie Melua: there is now a galaxy of stars in this genre but the patron saint of the open-air concert is Mr Boogie-Woogie piano himself, Jools Holland. By the time you've been to one of these concerts, you'll want to see the former Squeeze pianist knighted for services to men who are turning into their Dad. Rather than fighting your way to a mosh-pit at the front of a sweaty venue, you instead stroll serenely around the grass before deciding where to roll out your blanket and set out your picnic. There, already feeling more civilized, isn't it?

"I miss the days of pogoing, warm beer
and cold kebabs."

Apparently as you buy your tickets to these sorts of events you can also pre-order a picnic online. This is a delightful option, but of course you will find it far more sensible to make your own. True, you may well choose to grant the actual assembly of the picnic to the lady in your wife, and the only direct involvement you have will be choosing the box of wine at the local off-licence, but you'll oversee the process with the true diligence and authority that is expected of a Dad.

SAVOURY THE MOMENT

Firstly, you will make sure "there are plenty of savouries". You know how women will, given half a chance, fill the picnic hamper with cakes. Not only will this give you a horrible sugar rush – and the resultant, hellish comedown which gets worse with age of course – but then they will spend the rest of the night harassing you with questions about their weight, just as Jools is – surprise surprise – launching into another boogie-woogie demolition of a much-loved classic song. So, for every French Fancy they suggest, you insist on two rounds of smoked salmon sandwiches. Having satisfied yourself that carbohydrates, protein and fat are all nicely balanced in the hamper, you then chuck in the boxed wine and, hey ho, you're ready to go!

At the outdoor venue you are ecstatic. You should have done this years ago! As you wait for the first band to take to the stage, you don't have loud music being blasted out by a DJ as you would at the gigs of your youth; instead you have a soundtrack of people discussing babysitters and which B-road they used to avoid traffic on their way to the concert. Go on, admit it, you're really starting to enjoy yourself, aren't you? But it gets even better once the music starts. Why, if a particularly popular song is played, some people might even get up and dance on their blanket – after moving the egg mayonnaise sandwich and glass of ginger beer to one side, of course. This is like the rave generation but with beer bellies and expanding midriffs! Here comes your favourite song! Go on, really let yourself go! Boogie-woogie, boogie-woogie!

All that al fresco bopping to Jools's boogie-woogie piano will have filled you with joy. However, the modern-day musical scene just leaves you feeling empty. When your own father seemed disinterested in the music you were "digging" as a teen, you thought he was the most tragic being in the history of the world. Did he not realize how sad he looked when he said: "Sounds like a racket to me"? I mean, like, duh?! So let's have those adolescent sentiments echoing in our minds as we see you now, sat in front of the television, watching a music show and shouting things like: "Arctic Monkeys? Cheeky monkeys, more like! They only look about 12!" Or "BabyShambles? Baby faces, I'd venture." Or even: "Franz Ferdinand? Les Ferdinand would write a better tune than that lot!" You're a right one, you are!

Where does all this musical anger come from? Could it originate from a sense of disbelief that the music scene continued to spawn new acts and movements as you grew old and irrelevant? All those young lads with guitars, all those young girls smiling at them from the audience, all those opportunities you missed, all that resentment building... You're so angry it's a wonder you don't go mad and run, fuming, out onto the street and randomly attack people with your rolled-up copy of *Uncut* magazine. (Very interesting article about rare Van Morrison material in there this month. Now there was a rock star, kids these days etc...) However, anger tires you and so you settle for a resigned sigh and a changing of the television channels. For now...

TURN THAT RACKET DOWN!

But anger unexpressed is anger still alive. So, instead of randomly attacking people with old men's music magazines, your fury actually comes out when you hear someone else, anyone else, listening to music. Suddenly, you find yourself uttering that phrase you never thought would pass your lips. That phrase that really does confirm that you're well on your way to life's easy listening section. The phrase in question is, of course: "Turn that racket down!" You use it when others are enjoying music, watching television or playing a computer game. Even though your hearing is declining, every sound in life is suddenly a racket to you. Because where you once wanted rock 'n' roll, you now merely want peace and quiet.

It's richly ironic, though, isn't it, that you can even hear the racket that you are so keen to have turned down. Because with each passing year, you find your hearing is in sharp decline. Whether it's just a physiological problem – eg you are going deaf – or a psychological one – eg you are a little bit vague, what did you say your name was? What are we even talking about? – you can't be sure. All you know is that you no longer always clearly hear what people are saying to you.

Your hearing suddenly dramatically perks up, however, whenever you want a racket turned down. Which is pretty much all the time: when you're in a bar, shopping for clothes, or even in a restaurant, you can't quite believe how loud the music is. You find it particularly galling in bars. How are you supposed to have a conversation with your friends when the music is so loud? (Maybe that's exactly why they chose to meet you in this bar. Just a thought.) So you stomp up to the bar manager and demand they turn it down, for goodness' sake! Then, as you return to your seat, you get the horrible feeling that everybody is looking at you and thinking what a tragic, sad old man you are. Which is perceptive of you, because that's exactly what they're doing, Dad!

"I'll read you a story but only on condition that you convert and download my vinyl record collection onto this blasted thing"

So thank heavens, then, for headphones. As the years pass, headphones go from something you buy for yourself to something you buy for other people. Whether they want them or not. Especially if they don't want them, in fact. Because now they are more than presents, they are veritable weapons of warfare. Specifically, your war against volume. So hand them out to your partner, any children and indeed anyone else who lives in your house. Pretty soon, they won't even be able to listen to the news on the radio without you reminding them that you bought them headphones and, well, you'd appreciate it if they used them.

"Dude...if you want *'Dire Straits'* you'll have to try a classical music store"

They'd think you were an even sadder case if they knew how hopelessly confused you are by modern music technology. You don't know your MP3 from your X Factor. When you read newspaper articles about musical artists promoting themselves on MySpace, you assume that MySpace is something that claustrophobic singers demand when the stage becomes a little too crowded. You've no idea that it is a social networking site, partly because you also don't know what one of those is! The thought that people can download songs onto their mobile phones is so alien, terrifying and modern to you that merely thinking about it makes you want to hide under your bed for two weeks until all those nasty modern people have gone away. Not quite literally, but almost so!

The last time you tried to upload your CD collection onto your MP3 player, you descended into an afternoon of angry shouting, throwing instruction manuals at the cat, hours on the phone to the staff at the call centre asking what country they were based in and then, ultimately, the bitter taste of surrender, with your head in your sweaty hands. How impotent you felt. Yet again, technology had defeated you. Why not just let the robots take over and be done with it? At the end of the whole ordeal, fuming at a wasted afternoon, you headed straight to the pub and started ramming coins into the greedy gullet of the jukebox. The good old reliable jukebox. True, you enjoyed listening to *Money For Nothing* by Dire Straits and *Freebird* by Lynyrd Skynyrd, but your regret at all that wasted money the following morning was immense. So you scooped up your CDs and MP3 player, took them to your niece and – bless her heart – she returned a few hours later with every track lovingly transferred onto your player for you. Perfect. Now if only you could work out how to turn the thing on...

I LOVE ALL THAT JAZZ

Just as every man will experiment with facial hair at some point in his 30s or 40s – no, there are no exceptions and even if there are, they merely prove the rule – so will come the day when he succumbs to that other rite of nearly-middle-aged passage, buying a jazz album. For this we must return to the record store (oh go on, there must be another soft rock compilation worth buying) and wander furtively to a whole new section, possibly even a new floor, of the store. Terrified by all these new names and styles, you don't have a clue where to start. (You could have rung your Dad before setting off, but too late now!) So you are mightily relieved to find the compilation sub-section. Once there, you realize that your selection process is over when one album stands out perfectly from the crowd: *Smooth Jazz – The Essential Album.* That's it: take it to the counter, and home. You can't go wrong with a compilation, can you?

But hold on there. Not so fast. For there is another music-related retail transaction that becomes more and more common as you turn into your Dad. When you were younger, music was to be listened to and occasionally discussed. You might have flicked through the odd music magazine but that was as far as any reading of it went.

However, the sure sign of impending Dadness is when you prefer to read about music than to listen to it. So as you head home from the record store, why not stop off at the bookshop and pore earnestly through the music section? There's bound to be an anally written tome by some middle-aged, middle-class football fan that explains what their top five songs are, or their first 11 music/football analogies are. Or even a 15-volume series about rare Bob Dylan B-sides. Brilliant! Not to be missed, huh? You simply must own it – and now!

"What's this? It's got a good beat..." That comedy sketch

about the old man at the kids' party seemed funny at the time. Now, it would just seem wrong. However, it did brilliantly sum up why adults and kids should never meet in a musical context. This goes not just for parties, but also for any sort of conversation at all, really. So your teenage relative likes Hard-Fi? That is no excuse for you to bore them into a coma with a lecture about how Hard-Fi are merely a hybrid of Oasis and The Clash. He won't care and you will look silly. It won't make you more hip in his eyes, it will make you look less hip. *Much* less hip. Similarly, don't even bother telling any youngsters about the peak of your musical experiences – acid house, punk, Britpop, whatever – because it will mean nothing to them. Remember when your Dad went on at you about his youth? Did you care? No, you didn't. Well, when you witter on about yours, they won't care either. Yes, it is the same thing.

And definitely do not offer to "come along to a gig with you sometime". You will at best be laughed at and pitied, or at worst you will be named and shamed in *Kerrang!* as a saddo. Or in the *News Of The World* as something even worse! That's if you even get that far; more likely is that you'll be disappointed when you are turned away at the door and told no, you cannot bring in your smoked salmon sandwiches and box of wine.

It's not all bad news, though. For, just as a mid-life crisis or even pre-mid-life crisis seems to be inevitable for men nowadays, so are those days when suddenly you realize that maybe you're not quite as past-it as you thought. Perhaps you just walked past an elderly man, struggling and wheezing along on his zimmer frame. Having helped the old wreck across the road, you suddenly feel comparatively youthful. Oh yes, you're not finished yet. So let's leave you, on a Friday evening in spring. The emerging sunlight and the green shoots of recovery out in the garden have made you feel surprisingly invigorated, optimistic and – whisper it quietly! – youthful. Suddenly, you feel you'd really like to catch up with the modern music scene. It can't all be that bad – maybe there is some merit to it. Yes, you definitely feel like getting down with the kids, and if that goes well, you might even have one last crack at a trendy haircut, before the old thatch gives way and goes pouring down the drain as you shower. So, keen to discover what passes for hip these days, you flick through the television listings in the newspaper, searching for *Top Of The Pops*. Having failed to find it in the Friday night listings, you scour through the entire week's schedule, but still cannot find it. You're absolutely gobsmacked when you discover that it no longer exists.

Well I never did! No *Top Of The Pops?* Next you'll be telling me that *Melody Maker* and *Smash Hits* have folded! Well I never did, how times change! Oh well, it's Friday night and that means *Later With Jools Holland* will be on. As you live and breathe, of that you can rest assured. So if you can find the energy to stay up that late, you can get your musical fix after all, albeit not quite as cutting-edge a fix as you hoped. All together now: Boogie-woogie, boogie-woogie...

Chapter 2

DIY Till I Die!

The Beatles were responsible for some amazingly bizarre statements, with "I am the egg man, they are the egg men, I am the walrus" a particularly notable example. However, John and Paul called it quite right when, having listed a series of handyman DIY tasks in the track *When I'm Sixty Four*, they asked "Who could ask for more?" Granted, some people could ask for more. They could ask for a roof over their head, food, money and health for a starters. But I think we all know what The Beatles meant. They meant that for the mature man, DIY is not just a task, but an absolute religion.

Once a man begins to turn into his Dad, he exists in one of two states: doing DIY and talking about doing DIY. Fixing stuff around the house becomes more than an obsession, it turns into something that is little short of an addiction. You will whip out your screwdriver and tape measure at the drop of a hat. It's the "leave it to me, girls" mentality writ large, is it not? Before you know it, you can't stop talking about central heating vents, chipboard flooring and extractor fan maintenance. Oh, and let's not forget the hidden fascinations of artex removal. Boy, with all this patter at your disposal, you're good value down the pub!

Once upon a time, you wanted to be a hard man – you now want to be a handyman! And what a noble ambition that is. It will keep you busy *and* save you money. Because even with east European builders willing to construct and decorate an entire palace for the price of a sandwich, you can still save the price of a sandwich by doing it yourself! The appeal of DIY to a Dad is thus explained: it covers frugalness and paranoia (all workmen are out to get you – they'll rob you blind, burgle your house and curl an enormous, unflushable turd into your toilet).

I'M GETTING TOOLED UP

The handyman dream is not just a noble ambition but an achievable one, too. Face it, you were never going to be that hard man you dreamt of becoming. You could watch Robert De Niro, Ray Winstone or Clint Eastwood playing hard men in films all you like – indeed, for a while you did little else but watch such flicks – but that was as close as you would get to joining the army or the firm. So, as with your dream of becoming the feared, imperious midfield enforcer of your favourite football team, you had, with some regret, to leave that ambition behind. To become a DIY hero, though, is much more achievable – you can do it! You just need some old clothes, some tools and plenty of time. Old clothes? You've plenty of them by this time in your life. Time? You've got little else over the weekend. Tools? You love boys' toys and already own plenty – any you don't have, you can get if you need them!

Oh what joy! Rarely are you happier than when you are kitted out in your old clothes and are drilling, painting, sanding or fixing. You spend the entire weekend doing DIY and the entire week either thinking about or talking about doing DIY. By the time Saturday morning comes and you can finally "go and get cracking" on your latest task, it's like (wait for it, this will be a classic) you've DIY-ed and gone to heaven! Indeed, so excited were you about the task that you could scarcely sleep the previous night.

"I think my husband's DIYed and gone to Heaven."

Not that any resultant fatigue is about to get in your way – the sheer excitement alone will keep you going. That, and the tea brought to you by your good lady wife. "Thanks love," you bark, before returning to the fray.

Perhaps it's no wonder that men so enjoy DIY, because even the language of it is a glorious reassertion of masculinity: you *nail* things, you *hammer* things, you even – without wanting to get too saucy about it – *strip* things sometimes. Phwoar and double phwoar! It also allows you to clamber up ladders, dive down holes and do all other manner of boys' own stuff. It's what you've waited your whole life for! Therefore, you might pretend that you're annoyed when something needs fixing, but really, inside, your heart leaps with joy when the wife says, "There's a leak in the roof" or "the boiler is on the blink" because it allows you to tool yourself up, roll up your sleeves and go to war. The testosterone really flows once you get going on a task. There's also abundant potential for you to make manly sighs and groans as you execute the more physically strenuous aspects of the job.

Not that you're entirely immune to the idea of getting a tradesman in to do a particularly tricky job. However, from the moment he arrives through your front door to the moment he leaves, you are at his side, attempting manly banter – "Did you see the match last night?" – and also, crucially, trying to learn as much as possible from him about the job he's doing. That way, you won't have to call him back next time. However, he probably knows this is what you're doing and is deliberately only telling you part of the story. He knows which side his bread is buttered. Still, it's all good manly bonding, isn't it? He probably thinks you're a *right* lad!

THAT LAWN NEEDS EDGING

On a good day, though, you prefer to do any mending tasks yourself. Because only when you are fixing the house does it truly become your palace. However, the inside of your home is only one part of your DIY kingdom. Step outside the door and there is a whole new world for you to go and be a man in – the garden! Did your feet, in ancient times, walk upon England's green and pleasant land? Probably not – you probably weren't even born in ancient times – but you feel that intense spiritual connection with the greenery of your back garden. No more is the garden just somewhere you pop out to kick a ball round; instead it is an extension of your new-found, born-again DIY religion. Green fingers? Yes, siree!

So what do you get up to out there in your DIY mode? So much greenery, so little time! The starting point of your gardening obsession is the lawn. You swot up and become an expert on what height is best for the blades in your mower, you spend your Friday evening raking leaves off the lawn and, once that ghastly task is finished, you stand back, take a look at the freshly raked grass and say: "There, that's better."

But that's just the start of your lawn love-in. Then there is weeding, seeding and feeding. Oh, it's a poetic field, all right! There is topdressing and aeration. Furthermore, do you have "shade" grasses or not? Well find out then! If not, how can you convince your neighbour to trim down their trees, to allow the required hours of sunshine onto your lawn? You wouldn't have given a flying toss about these questions until very recently. Now, they seem like matters of life or death. Oh what fun can be had from a lawn, once you start thinking about it! And what is more fun for the man turning into his Dad than a spot of cricket? The sound of willow on leather, an ale on a warm afternoon. Why, you could construct your own cricket pitch out there. Lords, eat your heart out, for the budding Dad has his own shrine to cricket in his own front garden!

"The neighbours are complaining about you aerating
the lawn again."

Before long, you are leaning against your fence and having small talk with your neighbour about your respective
lawns. However, for the Dad, the grass isn't always greener
on the other side of the fence. No, to him, his lawn is the
best in the world. He will, therefore, enjoy his chat with the
neighbour, mainly for the one-upmanship opportunities

it offers. There will also be pleasure aplenty when they get onto the subject of a hosepipe ban. This is fertile ground for Dad-like indignation and bitter humour. "It rains every day, they warn us about floods, and yet we're supposed to be in the middle of a drought. It's health-and-safety gone mad, I tell you." Go on, linger there for a while and really put the world to rights. Accuse a few institutions of not being able to run a whelk stall. Conclude with a defeated, "Oh well, such is life," and go your separate ways.

As well as the lawn, there are hedges to be clipped and weeds to be eliminated. Here, you go into full action movie mode. Like your Dad did, you brandish the hedge trimmer with authority and menace, perhaps even giving it a few gratuitous revs from time to time. You'll show that hedge who's boss, that's for sure! As for the weeds, just let them try and show their cheeky little faces through the earth and you will be straight out there, hacking them to pieces as if they threatened the very existence of you and yours. "Leave me and my family alone, you little buggers," you will cry – in your head – as you eliminate them. Why, how your wife must admire you for being able to kill a small, green stem.

When it comes to pruning the roses, you leave that to your wife, just as on barbecue night she will meekly make a little salad while you burn meat. In return for leaving her with the clippers, you expect her to keep her nose right out when you decide that the time has come to lay a patio. Here, you get to really be your Dad. First, you sit down with a pencil and paper and make some preparatory line drawings, plotting the whole operation. An operation for which you will enlist the help of other men, all of whom will be only too aware of their subordinate status, as you order them about and make them do all the carrying, while you stand with your hands on your hips and a tape measure clipped to your belt.

Patios are as Dad-like as they come. Constructing them involves heaving stones around –what better way to return to the stone age and that pastoral naturalness? – and once you have built them you can have a barbecue. Imagine the Daddish satisfaction when you crack open your first beer on the patio and sink your teeth into your first patio-cooked hot dog. More of which later.

"I can't keep this us every weekend...next time get some advice on patio laying."

I MAY BE SOME TIME...

The budding Dad is rarely seen in the main body of his home because when he is not out in the back garden, blabbering on about his lawn, trimming hedges and massacring weeds, he is upstairs rummaging around the attic. There is something almost primeval about the feeling a man gets as he ascends the ladder up into his attic. It is as if he wants to pause, and tell his loved ones: "I'm just going up to the attic, I might be some time." What is it that gives him such an increased air of pomposity as he enters his attic? Could it be that, up there at the top of the tree, he feels like he truly is the king of the castle? Or is it merely a leftover sense of child-like joy at the sheer adventure of the moment?

"It's the big bad wolf come to tell the smelly pig his breakfast is overdone."

Bit of both, I'd guess. But whatever it is that takes the man up to the attic, the bigger question is what is it that keeps him up there so long. Even the smallest attic seems fascinating enough to keep a man up there for hours and hours on end. What is he doing up there? An, ahem, intimate kind of DIY? Even if he is, it can't be taking up all *that* much time, so it only takes us a small way to answering the question. There are only so many old photograph albums, discarded bric-a-brac and broken electrical items that a man can rummage through.

What he is actually doing, in all likelihood, is reasserting his masculinity. It will only take one admiring "Ooh, you are brave, going up to the attic" from the girlfriend/wife to encourage a man to keep returning up there. (Could it be that she encourages him thus just to get rid of him? Surely not!) In an increasingly feminized world, the attic is one of the few places where a man can stand proud and say: "I am a man." No wonder he spends so long, so many man-hours up there. It's a wonder he doesn't set up shop full-time, emerging only twice a month for a quick bath. After all, with modern technology and the like, the man could exist up there, live up there, eat up there and would probably be happier turning into his Dad in an attic than anywhere else...

...apart from, possibly, the shed! If the attic allows a man to indulge in marathon rummaging sessions, then the shed represents the arena of the rummaging decathlon. The shed is the venue for the Daley Thompson of the rummaging world. (Hey, whatever happened to old Daley?) Let's get straight to the point, in years gone by, the theory was that the man of the house would spend so many hours in the garden shed because he was, ahem, looking at dirty magazines and pleasuring himself, using his right hand.

Comprende? A news report about a man who got his genitals stuck to the padlock of his shed did nothing to dispel these theories. However, with the advent of internet pornography (absolutely never looked at it myself but have been told it exists) this notion is proven to be wrong because men still venture out to the shed and return several hours later, even though they no longer need a quiet venue to flick through the sticky pages of their disgusting little magazines. So *what* are they doing in there?

Escaping from the world, that's what. Or, more precisely, constructing a new world where everything is how they like it. In the shed, everything can be hoarded, nothing thrown away. Anally retentive? Get yourself a shed! Everything is collected and kept, because you never know when it may become handy again. Therefore, the shelves of the shed become like a mini-Manhattan skyline of jars full of – quite literally – odds and ends. True, it seems likely that you will go to your grave having not used that random piece of plastic that you have carefully kept in that jar for years now. But you never know, better safe than sorry. Because, after all, the potential sense of upset and repentance you might feel if you one day found a use for that random bit of plastic that you carelessly threw out is absolutely huge. You'd probably never get over it.

HOARDING LIKE A SQUIRREL

Hoarding and acquiring junk has become a major occupation of yours of late, has it not? Yes, thought so. No visit to a flea market is complete without you picking up stuff the worth of which might cause raised eyebrows among your friends and family, but is clearly absolutely vital to your very existence in your un-humble opinion. That second-hand framed photograph of the Rolling Stones – you need that. A soup bowl designed to represent a football – your life cannot go on without it. A slightly-dented, angled step on which to balance your shoes as you polish them – how did you ever cope without it?

The shed is merely an extension of all this. While the junk you accumulate and then hoard in your house would cause many people to pick up the phone and call for an ambulance to take you away and have you looked after by experts, the junk that you keep in your shed is even more bizarre. But nobody else comes in and so you get no complaints. And that's why you love your shed. Because you're the boss in there and nobody else!

You might even keep a compost heap just outside the shed. No, scrub that. You almost certainly do keep a compost heap just outside the shed. One of your more regular journeys is between the house and the compost heap, putting tea bags, apple peelings and other culinary offal into the compost heap. You probably haven't got a clue what you'll do with this compost when it eventually emerges. But hey, that's merely a small technical detail. In the meantime, keep chucking as much crap into your compost heap as possible. What do you mean, it smells? Who asked you Eh?

The whole man/shed love-in does still seem slightly peculiar. Anyone who has been in a shed during a rainstorm knows that it sounds like there's a herd of cattle tap-dancing on the roof. Equally, on a cold day, you might as well be in an igloo. Plus, there are all those spiders' webs. Not much fun at all to any sane or dignified person. But sanity and dignity become luxuries you largely disregard once you start turning into your Dad. So get out there and enjoy it!

Not that sheds are only used in a leisure context. Some men even use their sheds nowadays as a mobile office or studio. If you have a sideline in picture framing, writing or drawing, then the shed is the place to pursue it. The shed is also the place for you to pursue your dreams of becoming a millionaire inventor. Today the shed, tomorrow the *Dragon's Den* studio! Thus does the shed becomes a parallel world: part of your career is pursued here, and part of your leisure time is spent here. No wonder, then, that you cannot wait to get out there. It's like a bubble!

However, if you really value the escape-from-the-world joy that is life in a shed, why not go the whole hog and get an allotment? There you can sit in the shed without fear that the wife will call out from the house to check you are okay. Instead, you can switch on the radio, listen to the cricket commentary and totally escape from the stresses and strains of your life. It's like you are a colonizer, who has conquered a small yet precious strip of land. You're the Daddy here and nobody else is going to mess with you!

LET'S TAKE A LOOK AT THE OIL FIRST

Of course, to get to your allotment, I think you'll find that you'll need a car, and your four-wheeled friend also offers an abundance of DIY options. Having fallen for the stereotype of the dodgy garage worker who will rob you as soon as look at your car, you have instead decided that anything that goes wrong with your car can be fixed by your own two hands. Those garages charge an arm and a leg nowadays, so just imagine the money you can save by fixing it yourself. And – far more to the point – just imagine the fun you can have! Chance to dress up in a special uniform? Check. Opportunity to get really dirty and greasy? Check. Possibility that the lady next door will look longingly out of her window at you, positively moist with admiration for your manliness? Check! No wonder you love the smell of petrol in the morning!

First thing to do is check the oil. Then you must examine the engine coolant level. The tyre pressure should jolly well be checked monthly, too. It makes far more sense, you realize now, to address a small problem immediately.

It might save you a lot of time in the long run! Forward-planning joy, sweaty hands and manly spanners – no wonder you love working on your car, and no wonder your Dad did! You probably remember your Dad trying to convince you of the joys of car-fixing when you were younger. But you might not have listened properly. How right he was, though!

Now, as you turn into your Dad, you need someone new to pass the wisdom down to. If you have children, they will do nicely. However, if not, then there is always someone to hand who you can grab and bore to tears for a few hours. Any passer-by will do. Just fix them in the eyes with a potent glare and start telling them all about the fascinating joys of car repair. They might be bored at the time, but they will thank you for it in the long run.

Be honest: working on your car has become a highly-charged erotic spectacle. One is reminded of the scantily-clad ladies of *Desperate Housewives* saucily soaping their car as the hunky gardener looks on. Then there was Paris Hilton who more or less had sex with a car in an advertisement for fast food. That's hot! Likewise, there cannot be many real housewives who have not, of a lonely summer afternoon, found themselves getting rather excited about the image of a manly, greasy garage worker. You can't get better than a Kwik-Fit fitter indeed! So why on earth should you not kid yourself, as you waddle out there with your beer belly and your bald patch, that you are not causing dampness among every single woman down your street? As long as you believe they are getting off on you, that's good enough for you. Because delusion is one of those things that Dads are great at. That and DIY. Anything beginning with 'd' really. Whatever gets you out there and peering into your car engine.

Not that it is just about fixing your car; you also have to clean the damn thing. Indeed, cleaning your car on a Sunday morning becomes a routine. Why, your local community more or less measures what day of the week it is by how clean your car is. Filthy? Must be a Saturday. Clean as a whistle? Must be Monday. Somewhere in between? It's Wednesday, baby! Forget the calendar and Greenwich mean time and all that malarkey, the world really measures time by the cleanliness or otherwise of your motor!

Cleaning is more than just a bucket of soapy water and a big fat sponge. There is also waxing to consider. Again, it might be a bit of bother to wax the car but you will be glad of it in the long run. Everything to do with your car is about the long run; you are forever planning and looking ahead. Never are you living in the moment, but rather you are doing stuff that you will only feel the benefit of two years down the line. But, here's the thing, in two years' time you will be so busy looking two years ahead that you will not appreciate the benefit of what you did two years previously!

Confused? You should be: welcome to world of forward planning! Car maintenance is just one of many areas of a Dad's life where he worships at the temple of forward planning. The whole Dad ethos is one of being sensible, of being pleased in the long run for what you did earlier and of bringing some order to your life. Which is why the actual physical moments of DIY, gardening and car maintenance are only a small detail. The real joy, the actual joy, the momentous joy you are getting is in the planning, in the opportunity to be sensible. You old Dad, you!

Chapter 3

The Fairer Sex

Until the day you die, you will always have an eye for the ladies. However, just what that eye sees and how you process what it sees changes radically as you get older and older. Ladies will always be the fairer sex but you regard them differently. They see you in a new light, too. Once upon a time they saw you, if you were lucky, as a rampant swordsman. Now they see you as a cuddly old friend.

When you were younger, you might have actually spent time analyzing your relationships with women. How was the communication going? Were you spending enough time together? How was the bedroom stuff coming along? Okay, you weren't ever going to devote many hours to such thoughts, you're a bloke after all. But you did occasionally think how things were going in your love life. Now, that has all changed. Were someone now to ask you how things are going with your loved one, your response would be a very confused: "Not sure! Never really given it much thought."

As man approaches the age of the Dad, he grows tired of the whole "touchy-feely" culture that sees people analyzing their relationships and discussing their feelings. For the budding Dad, the ideal time of human history was everything that happened before 1997 when Princess Diana died and the whole nation cried. Well, he thinks, you girls can get all sissy and discuss your feelings, I'm quite happy being so uptight I could almost burst, thank you ever so much.

BLOODY WOMEN!

Not that the man turning into his Dad is entirely old-fashioned. Being a member of, you like to think, a more enlightened generation than your father's, you were appalled by his old-fashioned attitude to the fairer sex. You vowed that you would never be caught seeing women that way, because you're no sexist. So what a surprise to you when, the other day, you found yourself rolling your eyes and sighing: "Bloody women." Okay, this hardly makes you Sid the Sexist in itself but still, it took you one huge step closer to your Dad, did it not? Shuddering stuff.

It's one of life's cycles: when you were a boy you thought females were silly and soppy things to point at and laugh at, then you grew older and rejected all that silly sexist stuff and decided that they were wonderful creatures to be admired, respected and – whenever possible – slept with. However, when they reach their late 30s, suddenly many men decide that it's okay to start thinking women are irrational, silly things once more. Saying "Bloody women" is only one part of this. Associated phrases include: "Women! They're always creating dramas where there are none" and – a more simple – "Tut! Women!"

It's not that saying things like this proves you hate women. If anything, the opposite is true. It's the very fact that you have finally learned to live in harmony with the opposite sex that makes you feel comfortable about uttering stuff like that. You've come full circle and are now becoming more like a friend to the woman in your life than anything else. You've gone from not thinking of them in a romantic way, to only thinking about them in a romantic way, to, well, just kind of being a good friend to them. Cosy, and very Dad-like, much like an episode of *As Time Goes By.* Because after all, a kiss is just a kiss.

GO AND HAVE A NIGHT OUT, LOVE

Therefore, the day soon comes when you cease to look forward to your lady's nights-out-with-the-girls. Previously, you couldn't wait for her to have one of her nights out. On such nights you could either go and hook up with all your buddies and get totally smashed off your faces. Or, alternatively, you could have an authoritative night in. Order a curry takeaway, sink some beers and watch the football. As a man you relished that independence, chalking off the days to the next such date in her diary. And if there was no such date? Well, you'd encourage her to go out with her friends. "Isn't it time you went out and saw your friends. How are they all? I'd be happy to slip £50 in your purse." It was like prostitution in reverse: paying to get rid of a woman.

But now, you'd rather she never left the house. You want her around. That dinner won't cook itself, for goodness' sake! And also it's just nice to have a chat with her. She can remind you who you are, in case you forget! Seriously, though, it is when you and your lady become not unlike the couple from *As Time Goes By* – ie friends more than anything – that you've become even more like your Dad. There is, however, even worse to come. Some time soon, your wife will become more like your nurse. She will help you out of your chair; she will remind you when your parents' birthdays are. It is somewhere around here when your gender roles will start to become more and more defined. Thrown out of the window will be all those ideas that the lady can drive, the man can do the ironing, because we're all modern, crazy liberal people. Before you can say: "Help! I'm turning into my Dad!" you will find yourself serving out the roast on a Sunday afternoon, while your wife deals with the Brussels sprouts.

However – and here we come to the spine-chilling nadir of turning into your Dad – the day will come when all of these horrors seem like child's play. It is the day when a member of the opposite sex describes you as "cuddly". No words can do justice to how horrible, how ghastly, you will feel when you realize that you are no longer perceived as any sort of threat to the opposite sex. Not that you ever wanted to be a nasty threat, but you wanted ladies to think you were at least in the running of the race we call lurve. Hence the feeling of despair and impotence you feel when you realize that you're no longer competing in that field, and that you're barely a spectator. You can still flirt, for sure, but only in an entirely harmless way. No woman will ever believe that you are seriously trying to pick her up because... well... have you taken a look in the mirror recently?

Just try it. Go on. Go to that attractive young lady who has just started working at your office. Stride up to her desk, hands on your hips, and say something earth-shatteringly flirtatious such as: "How ya doin'?" You will find that however thick you lay it on with her in the flirting stakes, the chances of her taking you seriously or as any sort of threat are absolutely nil. You've turned into your Dad so you are so far away from being perceived as a sexual player that you could more or less rub your crotch in the face of a young female intern and she wouldn't take the slightest offence, let alone consider vigorously pursuing legal action. (Legal disclaimer: some of the above was written in the spirit of humorous exaggeration. Don't hold me responsible – particularly in court – if you take my advice literally and end up in all manner of hot water.)

"I wish for once you'd drop your
old male reserve."

Putting the chances of me inadvertently condemning you to lengthy imprisonment to one side for the moment, let's turn to how your taste in women changes as you mature. In those halcyon days of your teens and 20s, you used to love a good chat with your mates about which girl you fancied at work, or which bit of "top totty" you liked off the telly. Why, a night out was not complete without such chatter. You'd compare notes and either agree passionately "Yeah, I'd 'do' her!" or disagree violently and offensively: "Err, no! She looks like a moose!" A right bunch of charmers you must have seemed to anyone listening in. It's a wonder women weren't throwing themselves at you every day!

"I'm just not in the mood."

Of late, though, this has changed and you've become far less loquacious about lurve. Anyone meeting you would think you're – whisper it quietly – some sort of gay, such is your reticence to discuss the attractiveness of women. (They would, that is, if you didn't dress so terribly!) So why do you suddenly prefer to keep your counsel on this question? That old male reserve has kicked in big-time, hasn't it? This is a phenomenon peculiar to the male of the species. Women, if anything, seem to get even fonder for a fruity old chat with their fellow females as time goes by. A girls' night out is incomplete without fantastical chatter about squeezing Joe Cole's bum or groaning your face off as you writhe around in a haystack with Brad Pitt. Indeed, it's not unheard of for women's monthly magazines aimed at the 40s and 50s to include pin-ups of hunky young sportsmen and soap actors. But it's only the lads' mags that do that on the male side, and they're aimed at a younger market.

Up until now, I have tended to frame discussions in this chapter around the man who is in a long-term relationship with a woman. It is, after all, far easier to imagine a man turning into his Dad with a wife and tots or, at least, a girlfriend at his side. In contrast to this, popular folklore would have it that the single man remains forever a teenager. He gets hammered every night, shags girls left, right and centre and is, as the song goes, forever young. Therefore, it is thought, he is unlikely to turn into his Dad in a hurry. Perhaps it is they, these singular beasts, who are having the real fun in life. The Dad will normally sneer at such creatures, believing they are not only single and sad and lonely, but also perhaps lacking in some crucial department. So imagine the disappointment of the Dad if this turned out to be wrong and that the singletons were guaranteed eternal youthfulness!

"O.K I'm just feeding in your personal details for a suitable match..."

IT'S TIME TO SETTLE DOWN

Rubbish! Make no mistake about it, it is quite easy to turn into your Dad while you are single. Indeed, in many ways it is far, far easier. One of the road signs on the journey towards becoming your Dad is the day when, whilst discussing your dealings with the opposite sex, you say: "The time for mucking about is over." With the melody of the song *Father And Son* ringing in your ears, you decide it's time to find a girl, settle down. You decide that your days as a "swordsman" are over. This decision normally coincides neatly with the moment when you are ageing so badly that you've ceased to be particularly attractive to the opposite sex. It is, after all, very easy to settle down when there is not a single woman on the planet encouraging you to do otherwise.

So it is that your standards drop completely and you are delighted to hook up with any lady, just to avoid being left on the conveyor belt of singledom for ever and ever and ever. Your dreams of snaring your favourite female celebrity fantasy figure are long gone. However, all men retain a favourite female celebrity fantasy figure. So it comes as quite a blow – particularly if you are still single – when you see a photograph in the newspaper of her with her boyfriend. "What does she see in him?" you scream with a mixture of anger and disbelief. "He only looks about 12!" Of course he doesn't look 12 at all, but it is true that he is rather athletic and boyish-looking. In your advancing years, you suddenly become completely confused as to why a woman would find such attributes attractive. What is it that she sees in these young bucks? Why doesn't she prefer men who are balding, fat and bitter? Beats me. Tut! Women, huh?

"You misheard...I said it's a shame we're losing
our 'lido'."

IT'S A YOUNG MAN'S GAME

As the years pass by faster and faster, you can't help feeling that sex itself is aimed at a younger market. You've still got an eye for the ladies, for sure, but you're not so certain that you have the stamina for them anymore. It all seems like a bit too much work. To use an apt analogy: when you were a young man you could do 40 press-ups and then leap up and say: "What next?" Now, you're likely to put your back out on the rare occasions you attempt press-ups. If you're in a long-term relationship, this won't be the end of the world. The very worst that might happen is that you keep hearing suspicious buzzing noises coming from upstairs when your wife goes to bed early with "a headache". What's going on up there? Is there a bee stuck in the bedroom or something?

However, if you are a singleton and turning into your Dad, your lack of ability in the, ahem, press-up department is a terribly alarming development. So get yourself down the gym while you still can, my friend! Otherwise no lady will want to, ahem, do press-ups with you. After all, would you want to do press-ups with some old woman's face in your line of vision? Well don't expect any woman to be overly keen on the idea of doing press-ups with a man who looks like your Dad either.

Tut! Women, huh?

Chapter 4

Dadicated Follower Of Fashion

There is one item of clothing that, more than any other, sums up your increasing Dad-like tendencies. It's always been there, hanging on the inside of your bedroom door, but you don't know how it got there. True, you must have bought the thing at some point but that is one of the many transactions in your life that you've found incredibly easy to forget all about. You use it regularly but it's not something you ever get excited about. In fact, truth be told, you pretty much take it for granted. I write, of course, of the humble dressing-gown.

However, as you turn into your Dad, you become more and more fond of this garment. It's transformed from an anonymous, practical item to one of your best friends. You wouldn't be seen dead wearing anything else as you flick through the Sunday papers, loudly complaining about how many bloody inserts they shove inside the nowadays and how much "bloody nonsense" the columnists write.

Now, it's not just *wearing* your dressing-gown which you enjoy, which fills you with warmth and excitement. Now, even the prospect of going to buy a new one starts to become a bit of a thrill. When asked on a Friday afternoon by a work colleague what you've got lined up for the weekend, your answer used to be along the lines of "I'm planning to get totally rat-arsed and pull loads of girls," a reply that would be accompanied by a laddish, conspiratorial wink. Yup, he knew what you meant, all right. So when the day comes that your response to exactly the same question is "I'm planning to buy a new dressing-gown," accompanied by an excited wink, then you know the game that they call youth is well and truly up.

"Look out kids, here comes Basil Rathbone."

YOU ARE WHAT YOU WEAR

If you are what you wear, then you are turning into your Dad. The look you used to aim for was an urban warrior; now you are increasingly resembling a colonial warrior. There's no doubt about it. When it comes to clothing, we once again return to that central Dad word: sensible. For instance, nobody could deny that dressing to prepare for all weathers is indeed a sensible approach. So fair play to you, as you pack a mackintosh before every trip, just in case it rains. There's nothing even remotely silly about doing that and, as you stand folding up your mackintosh and packing it into your bag, nobody is laughing at you and thinking what a sad old man you are. Honestly. None of them are making jokes about you being an anorak, either. And in any case, when it is pouring down with rain and your fashionable friends are all getting their trendy clothes wet, then you'll have the last laugh, won't you?

IF THE CAP FITS

So that's good news. Even better news is that having fully surrendered yourself to the concept of dressing sensibly, there is no end of new clothing and ranges with which you can fill your wardrobe. Also, thanks to the "old school" and "Dad rock" styles, you can ease very smoothly and subtly into the realm of old men's clothes. So let's start at the top. Have you found yourself, during the cold winter months, thinking: "I think it's time I bought a hat"? I don't mean a woolly hat or a baseball cap. I mean a hat. Like a trilby, a fedora or even a bowler. Or maybe a corduroy flat cap. Hell, why not throw caution to the wind and buy a top hat? If the cap fits, wear it! And if it doesn't fit, ask the sales assistant for a different size.

(Just in passing: they're so unhelpful in shops nowadays, don't you find? Kids today, huh? Don't know they're born.) Some of them can't even speak English! And as for the foreigners...

"You're such a snob with your embroidered hankies."

Go on, though, do get a hat! It will keep you warm and cover up your bald patch. And honestly, nobody will think you look strange. (But you'll think that everyone is laughing at you, for sure. It's just one of those things; there is nothing more likely to make a man feel self-conscious than the first time he goes out in public wearing a hat. He could do naked somersaults down Oxford Street on Christmas Eve and feel less conspicuous.) Then in the summer, you can really let yourself go and get a panama hat. Anyone for a swift Pimms by the river? Pip pip! What a caper!

That's the old head dealt with; let's move down the body. So, how about a scarf to keep your neck warm? You know it makes sense! Scarves are fantastic and more or less compulsory clothing for the Dadicated follower of fashion. Forget about all those trendy designs. You want something that will last – after all, fashion is for the fickle young – so, when you get to the store, you head straight to the tartan scarves. Or if you are feeling particularly adventurous, why not opt for an argyle or even Pringle design? You know you want to. You could even grab a cravat, for the summer months. Go on, old boy, you'll cut quite the dashing figure!

All that cold weather will make you more susceptible to colds. However, your days of desperately scrambling around for tissues as your nose leaks like a tap are long, long gone. For you are now a member of that exclusive club: the handkerchief owner. These days, you wouldn't even dream of leaving your front door without a square of fabric in your pocket, for you to snot and gob all over when the mood takes you. Well it beats the improvisation that leads to you having – quite literally – greensleeves, does it not? Get a hankie, go on! Lovely stuff!

Having become a paid-up member of club handkerchief, you have a whole new world of Dad-like behaviour open for you. If you are wearing a suit, then you can fold your handkerchief into a pocket square for extra elegance. Just as there are eight ways to tie your shoelaces, there are a range of ways to fold a pocket square including The Presidential, The Reverse Puff and The Straight Shell. Something for everyone there, nudge, nudge, wink, wink! However, whatever you do, make quite sure you never borrow a handkerchief from someone else. Who is to know for sure whether they have soaked it in chloroform and are merely lending it to you in order to render you unconscious and stab you to death. That would be such a bore: there's something so final about death, isn't there?

Moving down again, of the many rules of science that govern the universe, I can only think of one that has never been challenged: that cardigans are lovely and comfortable. They are, in fact, the king of the comfy-clothing kingdom – and long may they reign, you might argue as your turn into your old man! As with the hat development, there is no need to fear that anyone is laughing at you when you wear a cardigan. True, quite a lot of people are literally soiling themselves laughing at you but don't worry – they are only laughing because they're jealous of you. In any case, just consider that the V-neckline of your cardigan is sending a message to your detractors – sending them, indeed, a flicking of the "Vs". They'll still laugh at you but never mind, you know that by wearing the cardigan you are combining warmth, comfort and flexibility. So there! He who laughs last laughs loudest. And puts his back out!

"Give it up Brian. It's a lost cause."

THEY FIT WHAT THEY TOUCH

Then come the trousers which can, for the purposes of this context, be summed up in one word: corduroys. Yes, these trousers – or strides, as you will shortly start to hilariously call them – are the staple choice for the budding Dad. If you end up buying an ill-fitting pair and getting mocked for this, you can always roll out one of the key catchphrases of this part of your life: "They fit where they touch." Ooh, your Dad would be delighted with you! There is something about light brown corduroys which screams: I am turning into my Dad! They are the fourth stage of man in his trouser-wearing life: from short trousers, to jeans, to combat pants to corduroys. Go and buy several pairs now. It's always best not to fight the onset of age!

However, when it comes to socks the news is slightly less positive. For a start, your ability to lose one sock out of a pair increases as you become more of an old fuddy-duddy – sorry, I mean as you advance in years. Just don't cross your legs during an important business meeting, lest you reveal one plain grey sock and one hellishly multi-coloured Christmas sock. Never a good look. However, lost socks are just the beginning of the hell that these horrible little blighters throw at you as you advance in years. You see, once you've stopped turning into your Dad and actually more or less become him, socks will become an even more sinister problem for you, plaguing your life on a daily basis. There comes a time in every man's life when simply putting on your own socks will become an almost impossible feat. (Feat/Feet! Geddit?!) All that bending down and aiming and co-ordination becomes such a strain that you won't even be able to consider putting on your own socks without calling a relative or a neighbour to assist you. Plenty to look forward to there, then! Sock it to me, one could almost implore!

"Mine does the same...a loud involuntary groan
every time he sits or gets up."

This brings to mind the whole grunting and groaning thing. No, I do not mean flatulence when I speak of grunting, nor of sex when I speak of groaning – though there is plenty of both of those in other chapters, happily enough! No, what I am referring to is the time in a man's life when he can no longer get up or down from a chair without emitting a loud groan. The same happens when he bends to put something down or pick something up: he lets out a loud "Oooooh!" Indeed, were a large group of middle-aged men to play musical chairs, the sound of all those men saying "Ooooh" and "Aaah" as they got up and down would make it sound, to a blind onlooker, not unlike some sort of gay orgy.

The clever man disguises his grunting/groaning problem through conversation. As he gets up or down from a seat, he will say something that is naturally accompanied by a groan. So, as he rises from his seat he might say: "Did you read that news story about that kidnap victim? Oooooh, it was terrible!" Or even: "Aaaaah! Speaking of vegetables, that reminds me I must buy some potatoes later!" Once you get started on this method, you'll find many creative ways to disguise the old grunting/groaning problem! Ooooh, there are plenty of ways to cover it up!

I'VE GOT A BLOODY BEARD, AND YOU HAVEN'T

When it comes to male grooming, there are plenty of things to cover up there, too. Another step down the descending ladder of Dadness is the day you grow a beard. Yes, you heard that right: a beard. A full-on beard. Not an ironic goatee, nor a week's lazy failure to shave. But a full beard of the sort that good old Jesus Christ would have been proud of. Long gone are those fears that you might get bits of food stuck in the beard and thus become repulsive to the opposite sex. You are now so settled down and past-it in the romance stakes that you could keep several meals' worth of crumbs in your beard and not a single member of either sex would have cause to notice. Go on, treat yourself! Open a beard bakery!

So let it all hang out in the facial hair stakes and grow yourself a nice bushy beard. It will keep you warm in the winter and also cover up all manner of sins on your face. Furthermore, beards definitely give a man a "cuddly" look and the faster you pull off the cuddly image, the faster you will turn into your Dad. Imagine never having to shave again. Oh, the sheer liberation of it! No more poncy shaving gels, no more brandishing a razor to your face. Long gone, too, are the days of stinging after-shaves. You will also save lots of money this way, and if you have ever met a Dad who doesn't get off on saving a bit of dosh, then you've met a Dad I've never met!

They say it takes about six weeks to grow a beard. As you get older, six weeks becomes a mere instant, flying by in no time at all. Once the six weeks is up, you can then start to trim it. You can also walk down the road with a new-found sense of authority. "Look at me," your expression will say. "I've got a bloody beard, and you haven't! Call yourselves men? More like mice, you smoothed-faced little sods!" Little-known secret: a man with a beard is automatically allowed entry into the Dad Club. Doesn't matter how old he is; the moment he appears with a beard, the Daddy doorman lifts the rope and says: "This way please, sir!"

Speaking of beards, I am sure you remember those days in your early teenage years, when you moved your face right up to the bathroom mirror in search of the first signs of facial hair? That little bastard couldn't wait for his first bits of bum fluff. Well, here you are again all these years on, pressed up against the mirror, only this time, searching for the first signs of hair loss. It's a truly awful experience, particularly the first time you notice the early signs of baldness. You desperately scramble your hair around, hoping that that gaping strip of scalp is merely the result of you sleeping a bit funny. But no, no such luck. It's not just that your pillow pushed your hair to one side. The pillow is innocent, so leave the poor thing alone. The truth is: you are actually going bald, you old fart. Help!

Baldness, however, is not in itself a sign that you are turning into your Dad. After all, some guys go bald in their early 20s and manage to look damn cool as they do so. (Though admittedly they are very rare dudes, indeed.) No, the real sign of impending Dad-dom comes not when your hairline begins receding, but at that moment that you stop caring about it. For as long as you are rubbing lotions into your scalp, necking tablets, cropping your hair and desperately trying any other baldness cure or cover-up that comes to mind, then there is a comfortable distance between you and your old man. However, the day when you shrug your shoulders and say: "Oh well, there really are more important things in life than hair," then you know the game is up and that you might as well get the pipe and slippers out and be done with it.

I MIGHT SLIP INTO SOMETHING MORE COMFY

And it is with slippers that we conclude this chapter. The word slipper was coined in 1478 – and once you start wearing them, most people will assume you were born around that time, too. If a dog is a man's best friend, then slippers must be on extraordinarily good terms with the item of clothing with which we started this chapter: the dressing-gown. The two go together perfectly. When Stevie Wonder and Paul McCartney sang *Ebony & Ivory*, the song was not a metaphor for racial harmony. No, it was a reference to how well dressing-gowns (ebony) and slippers (ivory) get along. Trust me, I've fact-checked this tirelessly and I'm definitely right.

Slippers are one of those things that come and go in your life. As a kid, you loved your slippers, probably owning a pair with cartoon characters faces' embroidered onto them. Then, somewhere around your teenage years, you literally gave slippers the boot. "Shoo," you told them. (See what I did there? Shoo! Shoe? Ha!) There was no way you would be seen dead in them. Nor alive! I mean, like: hello? However, there comes a time in every man's life – during his late 20s or early 30s, most commonly – when differences are put to one side, apologies exchanged and accepted and the slippers are welcomed back into your life. Just to prove there are no hard feelings, you'd add them on Facebook if they had a profile there. (Not that you probably even know what Facebook is, you slipper-wearing old sod, you!)

Now that you have to consider such things as not wearing out your carpet, slippers are welcome in your life. You love slipping into them and watching some television. Okay, so they reveal a bit of ankle. You won't complain if nobody else does. Whatever you said, whatever you did, you didn't mean it. You just want your slippers back for good. True, when you wear them you are increasingly resembling the cartoon strip character Andy Capp, but they're ever so snug, aren't they? The ones with a tartan pattern on them get you full Dad points.

Slippers are not just ever so snug, but ever so revealing too, as are all clothes. Clothes are enormously powerful and magical items: when dressed in old rags, a man will act and behave accordingly. Equally, if the same man dresses instead in an expensive, beautifully-fitting designer suit, then he will behave with the sort of class that his clothing demands. So when you lounge around the house in your slippers, and when you wear cardigans, hats and corduroys and the like, you begin to behave accordingly: that is, how your Dad would behave. Trouble is, if you're not careful, you will lose all control of your sense of style and will descend into such depths as considering buying a codpiece. For more help with this, see the forthcoming – and eagerly anticipated – book: *Help! I'm Turning Into My Great Grandfather!* (It's gonna be a bestseller!)

It all comes down to this: the moment in your life when you accept looking like your Dad. For so long you would rather have died than appear in any way like your father at all. You studiously studied him – is there any other way of studying? Ask your Dad! – and made sure that you looked different. You went to the gym to avoid becoming fat like him, you grew your hair to be the absolute polar opposite to his baldness, you wore clothes that were – in truth – aimed at guys a wee bit younger than you. You even tried to stand differently to him, such was your desperation to differ from Dad.

It was hard work but it was well worth it. Because nothing, but nothing in the world could ever be as bad as turning out like that old wreck. Look at him: the most desperate woman in the world could have been blinded and locked up in solitary confinement for 20 years and she would have to have overdosed on aphrodisiacs to even countenance the idea of a quickie with him. So: "no pain, no gain" was your motto as you left no weight machine at the gym unused and no copy of *Men's Health* magazine unstudied in your quest for differentiation from the dude you call Dad.

It was like every single task ever undertaken on the *Krypton Factor* rolled into one – that's how challenging and important it was.

Then one day – a gloomy, late autumnal Sunday afternoon most likely – you suddenly thought: "Weeell," – and you really would have spun-out the word like that, very Dadlike – "I suppose I could look worse." Yes, you could be smeared head to toe in cow dung, I suppose. That would probably look worse. But as long as you're comfortable with your new appearance, nobody is going to laugh at you... Dad (snigger).

Chapter 5

One Man And His Dog

It's a proud day in any man's life: the day he gets his first dog! Even if the man has no children, on that proud day he becomes in his own crazy mind something strongly resembling a Dad. All that "here, boy" and "good boy" and so on – it's positively paternal! Why, ever since he was a little boy and the family dog died – sob, there's something so final about death! – the budding Dad has been waiting for this moment. The moment when he is no longer the only drooling, roaring, flatulent beast in the household. The moment he opens the drawbridge and accepts a dog into his home. Which is, of course, his castle.

The Dad might choose to take a young relative along when he buys the dog, so the shopkeeper thinks that he is buying it to brighten up the youngster's life. The truth is, though, that the Dad is buying the dog for one person only – himself! I suppose really it's no wonder men love dogs. The terrors might on occasion chase after a squirrel in the park, lift a leg over the neighbour's flower bed or attack the postman as he comes up the garden path, but they're cute really! And then there's the dogs ... Boom! Boom!

But seriously, from their days as bouncy puppies through to the distinguished autumn of the doggy lifespan, the mutt is a must-have companion for any Dad. Indeed, you could be the father of 100 children (and what exhausting fun you'd have getting to that position) but unless you own a dog, a Dad you are not.

For in truth, dogs are the men of the domestic animal world. No man worth his salt would ever consider owning a cat unless he was either under colossal pressure from the lady in his life, or unless he's a bit, you know, peculiar. Cats are for lonely women, dogs are for men. ROAR!

"5 days ago I left the house, the wife and the kids for a short walk with Rex here and I thought 'Oh what the heck'!"

A MAN'S BEST FRIEND

The proof for this is there for all to see. After all, that BBC television show wasn't called *One Woman And Her Dog*, was it? No! It was called *One Man And His Dog* – and bloody right, too! Neither was that wonderful Jerome K. Jerome novel called *Three Women In A Boat – To Say Nothing Of The Dog*, but *Three Men In A Boat – To Say Nothing Of The Dog*. Likewise, dogs are not known as a person's best friend, are they? No, is the answer! They're called a *man's* best friend! We're beginning to see a trend develop here, I do believe.

Many a budding Dad has sat at the bar of some seedy hotel, moaning on to the barmaid about how his wife doesn't understand him. This sort of self-pitying sentiment is traditionally the signal for the man to take a mistress and embark on some sort of seedy, hide-the-credit-card-statement-and-hire-lots-of-motel-rooms-for-loads-of-noisy-sex affair. But the budding Dad, as we have seen elsewhere, is rarely one to cheat in the real world. No, he'd always bottle it at the last moment. So rather than taking up with a mistress, he will take up a mutt! For nobody understands a man like his dog does.

Your dog knows just what you're thinking, and just what you're up against in the modern world. So perhaps you might find yourself, during one of your meandering marathon walks, resting at a bench for a while, turning to your dog and saying: "Hey fella, it's just you and me against the world, isn't it?" Your barking dog is a paid-up member of your bunker mentality.

Even better, the dog isn't going to answer you back – unlike the missus, tut! – so he's the perfect companion for the budding Dad to blabber on at about DIY and how things are not as good as they used to be. He could even help you write a letter to your local newspaper about how expensive parking is. Or at least curl up at your feet as you write it!

WALKING THE DOG

Speaking as we were of meandering walks, for the Dad, walking responsibilities are not a regrettable side-effect of owning a dog. Rather they are a key reason for getting one. On a dog walk, the man can truly feel like an adventurer, heading out on some sort of manly mission. "We're just going outside," he shouts to the wife as he coils his scarf around his neck and leashes the dog. "We may be some time!"

What a wit! Oh, he's a right one, he is. Of course were he being more honest about his plans he'd say: "We're just going outside. Yes, this is the fourth walk I have given the dog today but I only ever got this bloody dog to use as a pretext to slope off for a bit of peace from you!" It's a cruel world.

Returning briefly to Dad clothes, dog-walking allows the man to invest in a whole new set of clothes. Scarves, gloves and hats – he needs all of these for his walks with the woofer. As for the hiking boots, well it's impossible to imagine him surviving the perils of a walk round the park with his dog without them! And then he's off, pacing into the distance with his dog at his side – or panting a few yards behind him – as if he is the most adventurous adventurer of all time! Parks, commons, marshes, even cesspits won't stop him! He might even consider taking a compass with him, and maps, and then noting it all down when he gets home! The Dad's Dog Diary – it's gonna be a bestseller, or at the very least a great thing to show his grandchildren when they are born. What treats he has in store for them!

MY DOG'S BIGGER THAN YOUR DOG

And who knows? Whilst the Dad and his dog are out on their long walk, he might even find himself wanting to stop in the local pub. It's not so much that he wants a drink – although if someone offers, well, it would be rude to refuse – more that he wants to show his dog off to his fellow boozers. For here, you can stand proudly as they, erm, examine your mutt, so to speak! Do not let the fact that you did not technically sire the dog get in the way of your paternal pride. At least I hope you didn't sire the dog. If you did: you randy old sod, you! (What was it like?)

The great thing about showing off your dog is that there is no end of dog trivia that can be imparted to an interested – or otherwise! – audience. If your dog is pure-bred, then you can talk about the history of the breed, its popular characteristics and so on. For instance, did your fellow boozers know that Pointers can be as much as 28 inches tall? Or that Silky Terriers originated in Australia? I bet they didn't, and I bet they'd be delighted to be told of this. So, just discussing breed facts should cover a solid 40 minutes at the very least. By which time it might be time for another drink. A swift half? No, I think a pint this time!

Even if you own a mixed-breed dog, do not let that discourage you from lengthy loquacity at the bar. You can lecture your fellow drinkers about the fact that mixed-breeds tend to be healthier and longer-living than pure breeds. I'm sure everyone will be relieved to know that fact. Indeed, they'll wonder how they ever got by without it, and will be scrapping with one another to be the first to say to you: "Wow! Do tell me more!" You and your dog will be the life and soul of the dog-discussion party. You old socialite, you!

As we've seen throughout these pages, Dads are competitive

beasts, who always want to get one up on each other. This is part of the appeal of the dog to the Dad. For you really will find cause aplenty for a bit of one-upmanship once you are a dog owner. As you lean over your garden fence, putting the world to rights with your neighbour, make sure you make him feel bad about his dog. Pass up no chance to indirectly remind him how ill-disciplined, feeble and just generally crap his dog is when compared to your impressive butch beast. It's great fun putting other people's dogs down. Metaphorically, I mean. The real putting-down must be left to qualified vets.

Indeed, canine competitiveness is such a popular pastime that they could probably make a television series out of it. It would be called *Pup Idol*, and would feature a succession of pot-bellied, grey-haired Dads parading their dogs in front of a mincing panel who all pretend to hate one another. The Dads would explain why their dog is the best in the world, and the viewing public would phone in – in their millions, I reckon – to cast their vote as to which Dad-and-dog duo should win the title of *Pup Idol*. A combination of Crufts and the *X Factor,* it's a winner of an idea – expect to see if on your screens very soon.

THE WIND OF CHANGE

Returning – with some enthusiasm! – to the subject of flatulence, this is where dog ownership really comes into its own. As anyone who has ever owned one would attest with some horror, dogs have been known to lift their leg not just to take a leak, but also to eject a potent gust of wind. Nobody enjoys this part of dog nature, and it's worth noting that Barbara

Woodhouse – god rest the old fart! – never managed to train this tendency out of any dog. The dog fart is quite an experience the first time the owner encounters it. As epochal experiences go, it's up there – or down there one might say – with the first time one changes a nappy, or the first time one wakes up in a pool of vomit after one too many ciders and cigarettes as a teenager.

However, flatulent fidos are wonderful scapegoats for the windy, budding Dad. Or scapedogs, one could venture if colossally poor puns were one's cup of tea! For once a dog is part of your household, any time you find yourself accidentally letting rip in polite company, you can simply blame the resultant stench on the little rascal. "Rover," you say accusingly as the hellish smell spreads around the room, "have you let one go again you naughty boy?" Students of the human condition will have noted that in this phenomenon lies the conclusion of the dog-blaming cycle. As a child, the *homo sapiens* says: "The dog ate it" when he hasn't done his homework. As an adult, the homo sapiens says: "The dog did it" when he farts like a beast. Cogito, ergo sum. Or something like that.

Pub buddies and fart scapegoats: dogs, huh, dontcha just love 'em? But this is all just the beginning of the appeal of these animals!

Given that the aspiring Dad has both a love of dogs and a feeling that if only he were given the chance to rule the world, all would be well, perhaps the two factors could dovetail – or, if you will, dogtail – rather nicely. Perhaps the Dad could use his love of the dog world as a springboard to put the world to rights! Forget writing letters to *The Times* or what have you, we're talking about real power here. The sort of authority that every Dad deserves! Now they'll listen to him: today, walking the dog along his street; tomorrow, walking the dog along

Downing Street! The sheer manly buzz of power and authority! Me? Past it? I think not!

"Do you have anything a little
longer in the leg."

DOGS ARE FROM MARS...

I can see it all now. The, ahem, "tail" of the Dad who went from owning a dog to running the country. Hollywood would snap up the film rights and the man could, in a sequel, go on to take over the entire bleeding world! Granted, I might be getting carried away. Just a little bit. But surely it cannot be doubted that if the dog-owning Dad had his way, he would make sweeping changes to the laws governing pets. Specifically, he would ensure that the superiority of dogs over cats is finally recognized through a raft of roverish legislation that he would sweep through parliament to popular acclaim.

Most significantly, he would repeal the Dangerous Dogs Act and in its place would be a Crap Cats Act. Under this law, anyone found to own a boring, lazy, vain, pointless cat – that'll be all cat-owners then – would be the subject of rigorous extra taxation. The funds raised through this would not go to any of those boring causes like health or roads or making sure pensioners who bravely fought in the Second World War didn't freeze to death in the winter. Instead these funds would be handed straight to dog-owners to recognize what we and our pets bring to the party.

You know it makes sense. Dogs are absolutely fantastic: they've helped us win wars, fight crime, and save victims of disasters like earthquakes and terror attacks. They are loyal, full of character and endless fun. No offence, cat owners, but your pets are a waste of space. If we relied on them to win wars, fight crime or save the stricken we'd probably all have died out years back. All except the cat, that is, who would be curled up next to a radiator like some stoned student waiting for *Deal Or No Deal* to come on. They say that curiosity killed the cat. I'm just surprised that anyone even noticed it had died.

Mind you, if cats are lazy then it's only because they are like their owners. During even the coldest of winter mornings, Daddish dog-owners are up at dawn giving their hounds a good walk whatever the weather, wearing their special outfits and pacing with such purpose that they terrify all passers-by. I suspect that if cat owners were called upon to actually do anything beyond spooning a bit of smelly meat into a bowl twice a day, they would quickly return their pets to the shop.

This rampaging, political Dad would also require all cats to be neutered. It would be pointless to let any more be born, once everyone realized how rubbish they are. Any cat-owners who were upset by this would be given the chance to own a dog. Then everyone would realize that the Dad was right all along and a statue of him and his dog would be put up in some park somewhere, for other dogs and Dads to bow their heads to as they pottered past. Respect, huh? It's hard to acquire but boy, it feels good when it comes along.

So now that the superiority of dogs over cats has been truly established, the wannabe Dad might find himself positing a theory that dogs are the men of this world and cats are the women of the world. So, if the politics thing doesn't work out for him, he could always attempt to enter the literary world. (The glamour, perks and money are second-to-none in this game, after all. No, seriously!) The name of his epochal, blockbusting debut? Why, I thought you'd have worked that out for yourself by now: *Yelp! I'm Turning Into My Dog!*

Not really! I was merely being humorous! (Is that what

you call it? – Ed.) No, the name of the book would surely be *Dogs Are From Mars, Cats Are From Venus.* It would help establish once and for all the superiority of dogs over cats and it would outline their varying emotional needs. It would be for many decades taken at face value. However, decades on – quite possibly after the author passed away peacefully in his royalty-cheque-secured palatial mansion – there would be some reviewers who would argue that the book was in fact an allegory. This school of thought would argue that the author was taking an Orwellian approach and that the dogs of the book were men, and that the cats were women. Kind of like an *Animal Farm* for misogynists.

This would then lead to widespread debate. Budding Dads across the land would argue about the issue as they nursed their pints in public houses. Some might even pen furious letters to local papers, outlining their own take on the matter. And as for barbecues, well, Dads would get so angry with anyone who disagreed with them about the debate the book created that there would be threats issued about faces being burned to a crisp, while the budding Mums would stop preparing their little bowls of salad and instead pull their men back: "Leave it Darryl, he's not worth it" and so on. Oh, how books can change the world!

However, it is dogs that really change the world. The world of the Dad, at least. A joyful animal, the dog is not just for Christmas but for life. They make us laugh with their funny games, shower us with affection and love, cuddle up to us when we're feeling fed up and quite rightly scream at the postman as he bring us yet more bills.

"My wife doesn;t understand us."

For the authority-seeking Dad, their appeal goes even further. For in this increasingly unpredictable and crazy world, there are few better ways to bring some order to society, and look distinguished whilst you are doing so, than to walk your dog around the park. You will exude authority and manliness. You will, in fact, be turning into your Dad with every step. So, if you have not done so already, go and buy that dog. Go on, you know you want to.

Chapter 6

Booze!

As a young man, you were quite the party animal, approaching every social event with the sort of hunger that only a wild and strapping young man can muster, wowing your fellow party-goers with your energetic repartee and tireless party capacity. Nowadays you are not the party animal: in fact, you can be more accurately described as the party ornament. Fellow guests are vaguely aware that you are there but you're behaving so tamely that were two removal men to carry you into the van, nobody would notice.

What made you suddenly become such a social goodie-goodie? It was probably the fact that the older a man gets, the more debilitating a hangover becomes. What was once known as the "morning after" becomes more accurately described as the "mourning after" and wreaks its havoc throughout the day and beyond. Oh, for the days of youth when hangovers used to be such relatively simple affairs. You'd awaken a little sheepishly in the morning, have a shower and by the time you could say "a full English breakfast and a tabloid newspaper please" you were well on the road to recovery. The whole experience was measured in hours and was normally a manageable affair.

However, as the years pass by the hangover goes from being a short-term event to something that can be measured not in hours but in days. You also start to suffer from the real killer: the hangover that becomes worse as the day progresses. You rise feeling surprisingly chipper. "Look at me," you chuckle to yourself as you shave in the morning. "I'm no lightweight – it'll take a more debauched evening than that to lay me out." Off you potter to work, feeling a little off-colour but still with a reasonable spring in your step. Then, some time around lunchtime, you suddenly start feeling like you've just swallowed a huge vat of poison and been thumped repeatedly in the head by a furious Amir Khan. By mid-afternoon you feel so wretched that you can hardly speak and you just want to go and lie in the toilet, have a little weep and collapse into a coma. A dehydrated and flatulent coma, at that.

I'LL HAVE A HALF

It is ghastly experiences like these that are responsible for leading you kicking and screaming towards that quintessential Dad behaviour: sensible drinking. A horribly boring way of living; for the sake of these pages, let's call this phenomenon "Dad drinking". Not to be confused with abstinence, Dad drinking allows you to stay on nodding terms with the proprietor of your local off-licence and pub. However, it also allows, nay commands, you to start forward planning when it comes to your alcohol intake. You take to having an extra large lunch on the day of a party. You start making absolutely sure you get a good litre of water inside you before even setting foot in the pub and then, rather than stopping for a kebab on the way home, you pop in the corner shop for a bottle of Evian which you must finish before turning in. It just makes more sense, after all.

But since when was drinking meant to make sense?

A key philosophy of the Dad drinking movement is: "Don't mix the grain and the grape." You know you're turning into your Dad when a night out at the local pub is not complete without you or one of your friends reciting the wisdom that mixing beer and wine leads to a horrible form of drunkenness and a more profound hangover. Never mind that this theory is actually contested by many scientists: if it's good enough for your Dad, it's good enough for you. For the dedicated Dad drinker, there is the companion wisdom that goes: "Beer then wine, I feel fine. Wine then beer, I feel queer." You get extra Dad points if you say this, unless you're in a gay pub.

Speaking of wine, have you recently begun feigning an interest in wine? Have you tried to brush up on bouquets' etc? That's because you're pretending to be your Dad!

Surveys suggest that by far the most commonly ordered wine in restaurants is the second cheapest wine on the menu. Coincidence? Hell no! It's all those budding Dads trying to combine frugalness with wine-sophistication. (But – neatly – not managing to pull off either of those things!) Next up on the to-do list for you will be deciding what to drink with what. This goes deeper, far deeper than merely having red or white wine with the correct types of meats and sauces. You will need to know everything from what to drink with oysters to what to guzzle at fondue parties. Then, there is the whole dessert wine issue to be resolved. Quart de Chaumes or Barsac? You need to know these things.

"Well I think we're all agreed...pub drinking games with bottled water may be sensible, but they're bloody boring!"

Another sure sign that you're entering Dad drinking territory is the new way you measure how much you've drunk at the end of the night. Wave farewell to those heady days of youth where you beamed with pride about how many pints you rammed down your neck and instead doff your cloth cap to the days where you will shamefully tot-up how many units you consumed, perhaps even making a physical note of it in your diary. Measuring your weekly unit intake might be very sensible but again I ask, what sort of person wants to put sensible and drinking in the same sentence?

Your Dad, that's who!

I'VE GOT A BUSY DAY AHEAD OF ME TOMORROW

It's not just the liquid intake of your evenings out that has radically changed, so has your whole approach to them. Where you used to anticipate your evenings out with wild abandon, you now feel far more equivocal about them. No longer do you burst into the party or the pub rubbing your hands with glee and saying things like "Come on!", "Bring it on!" and "Let's have it!" Now, you arrive a little nervously and within five minutes of your arrival you are quietly letting it be known that you'll definitely have to be on your way soon. Likewise, whereas the only thing that could previously spoil a booze-up was some bore insisting on going home at closing time and refusing your slurred insistence that you all "go on to a bloody club", nowadays you find yourself anxiously searching for such a dullard character so you can slip home as soon after 9pm as you can possibly get away with. After all, you've got a busy day ahead of you tomorrow and you'll need a clear head for it. Oh, you'll feel ever so snug once you are back in bed! Especially if you have a little hot water bottle!

"You have to excuse Gerald. He's not so much the party animal these days."

Not that having something to do the next day is the only thing that might put you off pushing the boat out at a get-together. Even merely having something important to do several days later is enough to make you insist on "taking it a bit easy" on a night out. It used to take you about 10 minutes on the phone to arrange a boys' night out. Nowadays, you spend more like 10 weeks arranging a night out and what feels like the same period of time recovering from it. You're about as socially spontaneous as a coma victim... but your Dad would be so proud of you.

As for your domestic alcohol intake, another sure sign that you're becoming your Dad is when your home contains within its walls bottles of wine that have sat there for ages, unopened. Previously, any alcohol that had the bare-faced cheek to pass your front door had as much chance of surviving unconsumed as a fox surrounded by a pack of hungry hounds. Now a bottle of wine can sit there for months, gathering dust and waiting for a special occasion.

As you become more and more like your Dad, you spend fewer evenings in the pub but probably more daytime hours – specifically Sunday lunchtime. You've kicked that Sunday morning football fad into touch – the stiffness the following morning was beginning to leave you almost paraplegic – and instead, clad in your finest woolly jumper, you meet with your fellow budding fathers for a Sunday roast and a chat about what you just read in the Property section of the *Sunday Times*. Then, weighed down by your roast beef, Yorkshire pudding and a couple of pints of ale, you go home and nod off in front of the television. You wake up in front of *Antiques Roadshow* and you're confronted not just with Michael Aspel's face but with the knowledge that without any doubt at all you are turning into your Dad.

Seeing as you and your mates are getting on so well over Sunday lunches in the pub, why not invite them over for another kind of fatherly feast: for that form of socializing that has Dad written all over it in 100-foot-high letters: the barbecue...

STAND WELL BACK, I'M GOING TO LIGHT IT

When it comes to the barbecue, there are two types of men: there are those who think the barbecue is the most wonderful invention and a great way to assert their masculinity. Then there are those who recoil in horror at the thought of sitting outside during intermittent rain, eating meat that has either been cooked to the brink of cremation or is so undercooked that it could hospitalize you for a week. Or in short, there are Dads and there are the rest of them.

For your Dad's generation, the kitchen was probably still considered an essentially female territory. Even though nowadays men are often to be found chopping and sautéing within the kitchen's walls, the barbecue remains the most authentically manly of culinary pursuits. Or so do Dads – and aspiring Dads – believe. So roll up your shirt sleeves, pack the fridge full of lager and cider, send the missus into the kitchen to make a salad nobody will go near: it's barbecue time!

It matters not how much havoc climate change causes to our weather patterns, nothing will ever come between a man and his barbecue. Once he has stood gazing out of the back window on Friday night, hands in pockets, uttering the immortal words "Do you know what? I think I fancy a barbecue this weekend," neither torrential rain, a hurricane nor a snowstorm is going to stop him.

As a young lad, your role in the barbecue hierarchy was clearly spelt out by your Dad. He might have let you perform menial tasks such as keeping an eye on those sausages while he nipped in to spend a penny. He may also have allowed you the privilege of fetching him a beer from the fridge. However, your subordinate status would already have been confirmed during the lighting-up process. The Dad will approach the lighting of the barbecue with the sort of care, attention and self-importance that James Bond might use while diffusing a nuclear bomb. Having watched public information films featuring men in flames, flapping around their back garden, he really believes you can't be too careful.

Go on, admit it. You too have found yourself hamming it up a bit while lighting a barbecue, haven't you? Thought so. Have you also been unable to resist the temptation to shout "Stand back everyone," as you light the first match? You're well on the way to Dad-land. You don't even need children to become the Dad of the barbecue because at any such get-together, the men will all gather round the grill and if you are the one who lights it, you know you've arrived in the land of the Dad.

However, you know that you've not just arrived in Dad-land but have bought substantial property there when you find yourself standing by the office water cooler on a Monday morning, cracking your knuckles and comparing notes with male colleagues on the barbecues you each had over the weekend. You start by asking them whether they used charcoal or wood, what is the best way to smoke meat and what marinades they used. Not only that, you genuinely want to know the answer. (Presumably you already know that it's mandatory to lie during such chats in order to make sure you emerge from the exchange as the king of the barbecue.)

If you've recognized any of the themes in this barbecue section then you can be pretty sure you're becoming your Dad. However, any doubts should evaporate when, on your birthday, someone gives you a barbecue apron as a gift. When that happens, smile appreciatively, put the gift to one side and just be grateful that they didn't buy you a pipe and slippers. Well, there's always next year...

WE WERE NOSE-TO-TAIL AT JUNCTION 6 FOR FIFTY MINUTES

Sunday lunches in the pub, barbecues... it's all go for you of late isn't it? However, there is one more key culinary get-together for us to consider. Everybody has heard of dinner parties. We've read about them in the supplements that come with the Sunday papers. We've heard mentions of them on Radio 4 plays. However, it's only when we are turning into our Dad that we actually start going to them.

Despite its name, what you eat at a dinner party is of little consequence. What really matters is what you discuss. The moment you arrive, you find yourself blabbering on about how you travelled to the party. Such conversations are fertile ground for Dad-like one-upmanship. If you can establish that the B-road option you took shaved a full 10 minutes off your journey time, you have effectively emasculated every single one of your fellow male diners before the first course is even served.

Other topics of conversation include mortgages, the weather, relentless quotations from whatever book you currently have on the go, personal equity plans and your workplace. You might notice during the early stages of the evening that the two sexes increasingly diverge to different areas of the room. Just like when you were teenagers, the males stand at one end, the females at the other, and the two genders will not mix until forced to by the arrival of food. One wonders what Germaine Greer would make of this. (I've never asked her).

"You are David Richards. Your chosen topic tonight is dinner party conversation and your time starts... now How long did it take you to get here and by what route?"

As mentioned, when you start being invited to affairs such as this, you know you're turning into your Dad. When you start enjoying and looking forward to them, there is no turning back. Before long, it seems as if you are either at a dinner party, planning and anticipating a future dinner party or recovering from a recent dinner party. (As well as the hangover issue, there is also washing up which can take days on end. Wars have been declared, fought and won in the time it takes to deal with the crockery alone.)

"It's the xmas party, Jane... let your hair down"

MINE'S THE TURKEY WITH ALL THE TRIMMINGS

After 12 months of fatherly partying, how can you see the year out in style? How else, but the office Christmas party? This affair used to be something you absolutely dreaded. Given your healthy social life, the idea of hanging out with that boring bunch of tossers from your workplace was about as appetizing as a mouthful of pig excrement. Back then, given how much genuine fun you were having in your life, the enforced fun of the office party seemed at best unnecessary. So you'd show up, quickly neck as much free booze as possible and then be hotfooting it to meet your real friends before *Hi Ho Silver Lining* got its first spin of the night.

Now, the office Christmas party has become one of the most eagerly awaited dates in your diary. And why on earth not? The drink is free, you'll know everybody there, the music will be familiar and the date and timing of the event is set in stone, allowing you to set aside a few weeks to recover from the rigours of arriving home later than 10pm.

You start preparing for it not just days but weeks beforehand. "Not long now until the big day," you say to your male colleagues as you stand at the water cooler, stretching as if it's a triathlon you are counting down to, rather than a party. "Or should I say the big night," you add before you all cackle with conspiratorial mirth.

And what mirth there is on the big night! From the moment Bill from Accounts appears wearing a Santa Claus outfit, you're in no doubt that you're about to have some serious, serious fun. Then, by the time the managing director has delivered an impromptu drunken speech praising the "three wise men" of the board, you're absolutely beside yourself. Then it's time for the disco and the chance to really show those youngsters how to party.

Mindful that there might be mistletoe on the wall on "the big night", you've spent the last month or so sizing up female colleagues for a possible festive frenchie. By the time of the party, you've a shortlist of potential targets but of course when it comes down to it, you know that if any of the girls showed real interest in you, you'd hide in the stationery cupboard, ringing your wife to check she and the kids are okay.

"Ah, I'm too old for all that, anyway," you mutter as you finally trudge home at midnight. The next morning you awaken with not just a hangover but a fear that it might be 364 days until the next social event you genuinely enjoy. Happy Christmas, Dad!

Chapter 7

May The Best Team Win

Once upon a time, there was a man who lived for football. Do you remember him? On the eve of the FA Cup Final he would have a restless night's sleep wearing the team shirt. He would sit on the edge of his sofa, drooling with joy for the entire 90 minutes of the match. That same man now only remembers the match is even being played when he watches the local news the night before the match. On the day of the match itself he has an undisturbed afternoon's sleep on the sofa, drooling with sleepy saliva for the entire 90 minutes of the match. He no longer loves football as he did. That's you, that is! It certainly lacks the punch of "You're gonna get your head kicked in!

IT'S THE TAKING PART THAT COUNTS

What made you suddenly so immune to the charms of the beautiful game? You can blame it on ticket prices, you can blame it on too many foreign players in the English league, you can blame it on Jimmy Hill quitting Sky's *Sunday Supplement* show but the truth is that you started going off football around the same time you began turning into your Dad. You can probably identify the exact moment this started: it was that day when your side lost the local derby 1–0 following a ridiculous last-minute penalty decision and your response was not foul language, death threats and a savage kicking of the cat when you got home. Instead, you shrugged your shoulders and said: "It's not the winning that counts, it's the taking part." Terrifying stuff, you'd surely agree?

"Bloody foul."

Just as all that running round a pitch for 90 minutes becomes less and less attractive a prospect the older you get, so does your passion for watching other people run round a pitch for 90 minutes diminish. There suddenly always seem to be "other things" to do. Check the aisles of any DIY superstore on a Saturday or Sunday afternoon and you'll see I'm right. That's what's causing all those empty seats at stadiums: the exodus of budding Dads from the football ground to "other things" – and shopping in superstores is one of the prime examples of "other things".

The mob mentality of football is what attracts many to the game. Losing yourself in a crowd, joining in with the chants and clapping, jumping up and down for joy when your team scores a goal (or wins a corner if you are a Spurs supporter). From the legendary Kop at Anfield to the Hampden roar in Scotland and the passionate songs of Newcastle United fans, it is the crowd just as much as it is the players who make the football match the enjoyable experience that it is. Not for those turning into their Dads, it isn't though.

For them, the football crowd is an unsporting, possibly even an uncouth, prospect. They still get along to see their team in action, though. Perhaps their favourite part of the season is the opening tie of the campaign. Arriving early, full of optimism, they look out on the scene, turn to their neighbour and say: "Pitch looks good, then." The pitch looks good? How much more could someone miss the point than this? If they went to watch the Tour de France, would they say: "The concrete looks good, then"? Confronted with the prospect of watching the Grand National, would they say: "Doesn't that jump look nice"?

"Pitch looks good."

WHATEVER HAPPENED TO SHILTS?

So why do they say it at football? This brings into focus the irritating Dad phenomenon of *needing to say something*. He knows the fact that the pitch looks good is irrelevant. He is also aware that his neighbour will already be aware of the state of the pitch and doesn't need his attention drawn to it. After all, they are both sitting there bored staring at it. Likewise, he doesn't want you to say other random paternal football phrases like: "Whatever happened to Peter Shilton?" However, the Dad thinks he needs to say something, to open communication with his neighbour. After all, it would be rude of him to not say anything. No it wouldn't! It's fine to say nothing if you've nothing interesting to say! Your neighbour hasn't gone to the match for a little chat with you, he has gone there to watch his team beat the opposition.

However, the Dad is no longer primarily interested in watching his team beat the opposition. Instead, he is too interested in beating something else – the traffic, that is. For another key phrase in the lexicon of the Dad-turning football supporter is: "Let's leave early to beat the traffic." So with up to 10 minutes of a game left, these supporters rise to their feet and make their way down the row, forcing their fellow fans to stand up to let them pass and obscuring the view of those fans who choose to stay to the conclusion of the game.

Imagine what drama these fans must have missed. There is no better goal than the last-minute winner. The stadium erupts into utter bedlam and the adrenalin rush of that moment is incredible. But that adrenalin rush will be entirely lost on the budding Dad. Instead of sharing that release of joy and tension with his fellow fans, he'll be trotting along towards his car as the distant roar of the crowd. Still, as long he has shaved 20 minutes off his journey home, they'll get over missing one of sport's most exciting and ecstatic experiences. That's how keen the is to beat the traffic. He wouldn't miss the teams shaking hands at the beginning of the match for love nor money, yet he is quite happy to miss the sheer joy of the last-minute winner. A funny old game, indeed!

Football also affords the budding Dad yet another precious chance to utter their favourite phrase: "*How* much?!" The opportunities to say this in football are manifold but top of the list is the replica shirt. No more do you excitedly queue up to buy the latest offering, instead you launch into a perennial rant each July about the design, the material and above all the cost of the replica shirt. It is long forgotten in your mind that you used to buy the shirts: instead you now raise a superior eyebrow as you slip on your retro-style football shirt. "This one will never go out of fashion," you say to yourself. No, it will never go into fashion, either. Plus, when you wear shirts like that you look like a mid-1990s Frank Skinner – and that's never a good look, is it? Not even Frank Skinner looks good when he looks like Frank Skinner.

Another football-related "how much?" focus is the ticket prices. Now, here the budding Dad does have a point. Tickets for football are ridiculously expensive nowadays. However, you lose part of your argument when you insist on leaving every match 10 minutes early. Some basic maths: Premiership ticket prices average around £50 per match at the time of writing. So if you attend just 15 matches per season, you're going to be set back £750 for the tickets alone. (We'll leave aside for the moment the booking fees, etc, but you can be sure the budding Dad is damn furious about them, too.) But by leaving each match 10 minutes early, you're throwing away one-ninth of what you're shelling out. So before berating the ticket office staff with your cry of "how much?", have a think about how much money you are wasting by leaving matches early. Go on, think about it!

"We're still crazy then..."

The slightest tinkering in the game completely throws you. You don't know your golden goal from your Champions' League group stage and so you spend much of the game asking whichever poor soul you are watching it with what might happen next, thus never being at all aware of what is happening now. "Will this go to a replay or penalties?" you ask. "Neither," he replies, "it's a league game and we're losing 10–0." Seriously, though, you go from being a football fan to a football flounderer, utterly lost in what you see as a totally brand new ball game. Still, to be fair it happens to the best of us. Even a BBC radio commentator managed to declare that Lewis Hamilton's car was travelling worryingly slowly in a race, unaware that he was watching a slow-motion television replay.

Sporting nostalgia really kicks in when you are turning into your Dad. For some reason – must be to do with the masculinity of the roles – the players who most arouse rose-tinted visions in the eyes of football fans are combative players like central midfielders and centre-backs. You've no doubt that Ron Harris and Norman Hunter are so much harder than the current crop of players. This is probably true but also irrelevant: we're talking about football, not boxing. Banging on and on about how hard footballers are is as pertinent as discussing how good boxers are at scuba diving. Given the various rule changes, including the outlawing of the tackle from behind, and the increasing strictness of referees, this debate becomes less relevant with each passing year. In any case, much as I hesitate to engage on this level, let's think what would happen if John Terry had a scrap with an in-his-prime Ron Harris. Terry would batter him, wouldn't he? Not just because of physical bulk but due to his superior fitness. So please, leave your misty eyes at home! Or at least get them tested, you old fart!

"You daft cow... I said I needed some
company as I was out for a duck"

It's often said that some people talk a good game and that can certainly be said of many of the pundits you find on sporting broadcasts nowadays. They sit there with their posh suits and their fake tans and jabber on and on. Some of them even make sense. As the years pass by, the male football fan might find himself increasingly looking forward to hearing the thoughts of Alan Hansen, Andy Gray and the rest more than they look forward to watching the actual match. It's a strange parallel world where the discussion of something is more important than the something itself. However, you have to have the something to discuss the something. The something is a necessary evil that must take place in order to discuss the something. Otherwise there is nothing. Or something like that, anyway.

IT JUST *IS* CRICKET

As we've seen, playing football on a Sunday morning has now proved to be far too exhausting for you but you still miss the banter of it all. So it is that you take that key budding Dad step and join the local cricket club. Oh, the banter you have with your fellow players and the adventures you have while on the road together. The time that it rained and rained and you never got to even start the match but all ended up in the pub, the time "Shagger Bob" forgot to bring the pads and what about the after-effects of that curry when you'd beaten that team in Nottingham? Oh, you could tell us some stories.

"I've just watched your *'Topless Tennis'*
DVD... it's not cricket!"

Here is where the divergence between a Dad's vision of his exploits and the rest of the world's view of his activities shows itself particularly starkly. He might think by joining a cricket club he is becoming something of a desirable athlete, a sporting pin-up no less. But really, membership of a village cricket club is hardly going to have the ladies peeling down their pants, is it? Heck, membership of the English national cricket team is hardly a guarantee of sexual offers, I wouldn't have thought. So you old farts rambling around your local green are hardly going to be fighting them off.

However, even given the I'm-raising-the-white-flag despair that joining a cricket club entails, it is still a relatively youthful pursuit compared to the, erm, daddy of Dad sports that is golf. Given the horrific elitism of golf clubs, they become a huge draw to men as they turn into their Dads. After all, as Groucho Marx said, nobody wants to join a club that wants them as a member. Plus, the chance to wear "sports casual" gear and stroll around the course is too much to resist for many a man as he turns into his father. And as for the terminology, it's full of birds and bogeys – perfect!"

IT ALWAYS BLOODY RAINS

Perhaps the ultimate Daddy relationship with sport, though, comes not with football, nor cricket, not even golf – but with tennis. Not playing it of course – why, you get tired just thinking about it, and you really don't want to put your back out again – but watching it. As I live and breathe, you might say, there is nothing that defines a man as more like his Dad than watching Wimbledon on the BBC each year. And once you've silently perved over the young female tennis players, and said that the young male ones only look about 12, you are most of the way there.

However, for full Daddy sporting marks, you also need to sigh, raise your eyes to the heavens and say: "Oh well, if it's Wimbledon fortnight, then it's bound to rain." Then, as the first drops of rain fall, fold your arms and say: "See! Told you so!" and sit back smugly. Everyone will think you're awfully clever! No, really.

From playing football to sleeping in front of the football to playing golf, truly the sport of the sleeping, a man's sporting life goes through plenty of changes as he grows older. Before long he has slumped from the Premier League of youth to the Vauxhall Conference of Dad-dom. Going down, going down, going down!

Chapter 8

Look After The Pennies...

It can be heard in shops across the land. It is the cry of every Dad who has ever set foot inside a shop, or indeed any retail environment. It goes something like this: "HOW much?!" So get practising, for this phrase will be like a mantra for you each and every time you go shopping, for the rest of your life. As you turn into your Dad, you become increasingly angry and perplexed by pricing. There is literally no product in the universe whose price you are not amazed and angered by. Even when you pluck something from the bargain bucket, during the height of the January sales, a product that has been reduced and reduced and reduced in price, you will still be utterly unable to believe that it costs so much.

So you must scream out, incredulously, when you discover the price of any item. Then, to add variance and wit to the episode, when the final price of your shopping is revealed by the till assistant, say: "Is that the time?" If executed correctly, this can be literally hilarious. "12.50 please," says the till assistant, blissfully unaware of the humour that is merely round the corner. "Is that the time?" you reply. They'll be rolling in the aisles, so they will. Rightly so, because you're a right one, you are! A right Dad, that is!

So prepare yourself, for the whole shopping experience is going to change radically for you. Granted, shopping has never been a particularly masculine pursuit. Rare is the man who says such bloodcurdling things as "I shop until I drop". And even those who do say that would surely go on to add: "And I drop within three minutes of starting", to jovial, manly laughter all round. Previously healthy, energetic male beasts can be turned into lethargic flops the moment they enter a shop. It's not just when they're accompanying the missus, and being asked time and time again whether her "bum looks big in this". No, even shopping for you has always been a drag. Particularly buying trousers, which seems to be something men will avoid like the plague for years, before running into a shop and buying three pairs at once, then getting home, hanging them up, wiping sweat from their brows and saying to themselves: "Yup, they'll do me for another few years."

And all this customer craziness before you even begin to turn into your Dad! There's so much more to come!

Set aside, for instance, much longer for every shopping trip. As well as screaming "HOW much?" at the top of your lungs every time you go anywhere near a shop, you will also find yourself adding a number of time-consuming new things to your shopping trips. Chief among these is the habit of comparing prices in supermarkets. Now, when buying something expensive and important (a house, say, or maybe even a car) it is perfectly reasonable to pay great attention to the prices of the various properties or models you are considering buying. Indeed, it would be insane not to – even the dragons on the BBC show *Dragons' Den* have been known to haggle over half a percentage of a company and it's not like they haven't got a few bob in the bank. In fact, it could be argued that it is precisely because they haggle over half a percentage here and there that they are rich, but let's stick to the topic.

"And the beauty of these low energy bulbs is they're so pathetically dim that if your wife or kids leave them on in an empty room you won't even notice."

WE'LL SAVE A FORTUNE IN THE LONG RUN

So, looking back to before we strayed off-topic, we're agreed that it is sensible to compare prices when splashing out for a home or a car, right? However, how long can one justifiably – or even sanely – spend considering and comparing the prices for different light bulbs, or cucumbers or brands of margarine? Remember, we have just the one life on this planet – okay, some people would argue with that but again, let's stay on topic – so how much of it do you want to waste weighing up the differing prices of everyday supermarkets? Lots of it, would seem to be the answer. Go to any store nowadays and you'll see hordes of men holding different versions of the same products in their hands, doing mental arithmetic. "If I buy this brand of potato, it might cost more now, but in the long run we'll save 2p per pound," they are thinking. True, they'll save 2p per pound but they've already lost several minutes of their life. Which do you think is most valuable? Okay, the 2p per pound. Fair enough, at least you're honest!

Another development worth noting is your increasing awareness of offers. Anything that is on "3 for 2" in the supermarket immediately grabs your notice, even on the extremely rare occasions when it is subtly advertised. You are the human equivalent of the metal detector when it comes to such offers. You'd be more or less willing to buy something you didn't want, just to have that father-like glow of pride at putting another "3 for 2" notch on your belt. "Got the bastards," you think silently, as the shop owner laughs all the way to the bank. Similarly, the moment you set foot inside a supermarket, you head straight for the reduced section. There, you browse through the foodstuffs that are about to pass their sell-by date and grab as many as you can.

"Have you got any bin ends to go with the road kill?"

NEVER DID ME ANY HARM

However, the sell-by date has become something of a negotiable affair for you, has it not? Thought so. You are now quite happy to risk it and eat something that has not just passed its sell-by date but also grown a small but thriving community of mould over it. "Never did me any harm," you shrug as you chuck some mouldy food down your gullet. The work colleagues who have to use the same lavatory facilities the following day might politely beg to differ. But hey-ho, you saved some money – who cares if your shit smells like, well, shit?

Another way of annoying other human beings that you can adopt as you turn into your Dad is by becoming overly chatty with the man or woman on the till. The potential for small talk here is immense, so try and strike up as mundane a conversation with them as you can manage. For full effect, do this when you are at the front of a very long queue. Chat away with the checkout guy or girl about, say, the weather for a while. As you sense the queue behind you getting increasingly frustrated, do not give in. After a while, say chirpily: "Oh well, I mustn't hold you up." Good fun!

Fun as these games are, though, it's all about price comparison for you. Just as you compare prices in the supermarket, so do you have your own price comparison system behind closed doors. Many a Sunday afternoon has seen you forego the live football on television and instead settle down at your dining room table with a pile of bank statements and your cheque books. Thus ensues a methodical afternoon of comparing one with another. You sit there, reading glasses balanced on the end of your nose, a suspicious, concentrating glare upon your face, checking and double-checking that nobody has ripped you off. Because if they have, you will bloody well notice, you will. And then you'll really give them what for!

However, your suspicion over banks is a mild, tame beast when compared with the raging dubiosity you feel towards restaurant owners and the vagabonds they employ as waiters. Today's younger generation seem to "eat out" more than previous generations did. You too probably hopped off to Pizza Express or Wagamama quite happily until recently. Or maybe you fancied a Thai or a gastropub? Whatever your particular taste in food, the point is that you were happy to eat out and the extra expense could go hang as far as you were concerned. Maybe you'd even stop off for a drink or two on the way home? Rock, and also roll for goodness sake!

IT'S A SWIZZ

Now, though, you are rarely seen dining out. You've come to the conclusion that eating out is like throwing money down the drain. Pizza Express? You'd be just as happy stopping in with a cheese and tomato sandwich on brown bread, thanks very much all the same. Wagamama? Waste-amama more like! Pizza Express? Price Excess, you'd say! However, on the odd occasions you do eat out, your sense of financial suspicion is at its highest. Your rip-off radar is rotating and flashing like mad. Nobody is going to get anything past you in a hurry! The way to a man's heart is through his stomach, but that doesn't mean they'll be able to con you!

First to set off your radar is the waiter. You're sure he's trying to rip you off from the moment you arrive. From the table he shows you to – it's hot here, maybe he wants us to order extra drinks? – to the way he takes your order – was that a sneer as you asked for tap water? – you are almost convinced he is out to get you. The great writer Kingsley Amis always believed that waiters were conspiring to arrive at the table immediately before he delivered the punchline to his stories. But with you, the suspicion is almost entirely financial. They'll fleece you if you relax for a moment, you suspect. However, any doubts about his desire to fleece you evaporate when the waiter brings the bill. You sit perusing it, glasses perched on the end of your nose again, desperate to find evidence that an extra drink or side dish has been illegally inserted by that shabby little man who calls himself a waiter. Your favourite suspicion is that he is trying to get the service charge out of you twice.

By the time you get home, you are so exhausted by all that vigilance that you cannot remember whether you enjoyed what you ate, nor even what you ate. And even though you quadruple-checked the bill, you still cannot quite give up your doubts that something "a little untoward" went on. With your digestive system turning into your Dad's, all that unfamiliar food will probably repeat on you all night. You'll probably get up a fair few times for some belching, buttock-scratching walks along the landing. Then, too, you will wonder whether that bastard little waiter ripped you off. Or, the way your actual guts are feeling, attempted to mildly poison you. Either way, you will be dining at home in future.

THE WINDS OF CHANGE

Speaking of digestive systems, I feel in all conscience that we can no longer avoid the subject of flatulence. It's said that a dog is a man's best friend, which is probably true. However, farts must come a very close second. I'm amazed there has never been a television show called *One Man And His Fart*, because it would be an absolute winner in the ratings battle. How we males love our farts: as babies we let rip without caring who else is in the room. As children we do the same. Hell, even as adults many of us are happy to lift a leg and emit a potent gust, whatever company we are in. Some of us may have even lit a fart and, aside from the singed pubes, found it a rewarding experience. It's all good fun.

However, as a man reaches the Dad period of his life, his relationship with wind takes a sinister turn for the worse. We all know the maxim that children should be seen and not heard, but in the case of the budding Dad's flatulence, it is more of a case of older men are smelt and not heard. Where you used to be able to wake up half the neighbourhood every time you let rip, your farts are now quieter affairs. Why, just the other day as you were making your breakfast, you clenched your face and expected a thunderous din to emerge from deep in your bowels. Instead, a scarcely audible hiss emerged. You were probably inconsolable with disappointment.

"I thought from the noises when you're in ours we already had one."

As the volume of a man's farts decreases, so does the awfulness of the smell increase spectacularly. It gets worse and worse whatever you eat, but certain foodstuffs are particular offenders. Don't even go near hummus and falafel unless you are planning to be arrested on suspicion of biological terrorism. As things get even more sickening, your partner finds herself purchasing charcoal tablets to try and bring some sort of odour-order to your lives. Terrible times and a terrible topic, so let's move on. I apologize for bringing it up in the first place. It's a load of hot air, really!

WASTE NOT, WANT NOT

So where were we? Oh yes, you'll be dining at home from now on. Dining at home too has plenty of potential to impose thriftiness. Never again will there be any leftovers thrown into your bin. You will either force-feed them to your children, or wrap them up and stick them in the fridge, or take them down to your compost heap. Waste not, want not, people! Even an apple core or pizza crust will get thrown into the dog's food bowl. How proud your Dad would be to see you now, thrusting that last piece of pie down a child's throat, giving Brussels sprouts to a soon-to-be incontinent dog, or throwing potato peelings onto the compost heap and pacing indignantly back to the house. That's my boy!

This spendthrift mentality was all backed up by being part of the loan generation. There are always a long line of people willing to lend money and always an even longer line of people willing to borrow it. Living beyond your means is more or less a way of life for younger people now. Beginning at university, they build up a debt and then it is only too easy to borrow that bit more, or get that extra credit card. Thanks to all those horrendous advertisements on cable television, there is a steady queue of nasty sods ready to help plunge you even further into debt! The younger generation is the generation of debt, after all! But as you become your Dad, you fall in line with the old maxim: neither a borrower, nor a lender be. Now, it's not all about credit cards for you; instead, the storecard is your new flexible friend. You become obsessed with how many points you earned during your last supermarket visit. This becomes a badge of honour to you, something to show off about down the pub. My goodness, they'll be jealous of you for the tally you have amassed.

How will you spend all those points you have earned? I would say that a jumper might be a wise investment. Why? Because of your new-found distrust of central heating, that's why! It's a fact that at any given moment in the day, somewhere in every city a man is switching off the central heating in his home. It could be sub-Siberian temperatures outside and inside, yet you will choose to eschew the modern wonders of radiators warming your house. "What do you mean, cold?" you will ask anyone who complains. "It's boiling in here! Go and put another jumper on if you're that cold! Do you think I'm made of money?"

Why is it that you keep asking people if they think you're made of money? It cannot surely be a purely rhetorical question; presumably you actually want to know if people think you're made of money? The answer, my friend, is that nobody thinks that. They just don't want to freeze to death during their sleep. They simply want to be able to warm up to such an extent that icicles stop growing out of their noses. But they shouldn't hold their breath because just as you cannot teach an old dog new tricks, neither can you teach an old Dad new attitudes to central heating. As far as you are concerned, central heating is a sinister, money-wasting thing and that's all there is to it. End of conversation. It's a load of hot air, really!

Not just sinister and money-wasting, but dangerous too. For just as frugality increases in men as they age, so does domestic paranoia. Men become obsessed with the idea that their boiler is going to explode (unlikely, particularly if you hardly ever turn it on!); their freezers are going to cause a tsunami during the night (well, at least it would extinguish the fire caused by the exploding boiler) and any candles that are alight are going to burn the whole neighbourhood down. It's little wonder, then, that the Dad wants the boiler switched off all the time. Who wants to pay extra money to be taken to their certain death? Not you, and not your Dad! Like father, like son!

It's the same with lighting. From the moment the sun sets, you become a spectral figure, haunting all floors of your home and switching off lights. You are utterly indiscriminate and shameless about this. You will think nothing of walking into a room full of people and switching off the light, without asking them or even acknowledging they are there. Off goes the light and you stride off as if there had been nobody in there in the first place. You've no idea how much it costs to have light bulbs on but you imagine that it must cost, ooh, something like £5 million per hour. Easily. Everyone wants your money off you.

Now, let us take a quick peek into your larder. There is plenty of useful stuff in there, for sure. But what are all these tinned, long-life products doing in there? They are absolutely cluttering up the larder, aren't they? In every man somewhere is a wannabe soldier. (Apart from, of course, real soldiers. They don't have a wannabe soldier anywhere in them. That would be ridiculous.) So when you combine a man's growing sense of paranoia with his military aspirations, and then chuck in the headlines about how weather or dirty bombs are going to kill us all now, you end up with a man whose larder is full of long-life products. Among these are bottled water. Woe betide anyone who tries to drink one of these bottles. They are being kept there in case of Armageddon and so must not be opened until we're all dead. Hey, I didn't say this all made sense.

This combination of a military mindset and a frugal tendency occurs again when the lady in your life asks you what she should get from the supermarket. "Just basic rations," you snap back, your voice slightly deeper than usual. She might roll her eyes to the sky and walk off giggling to herself but that doesn't mean she doesn't take you seriously. You're the man of the house and everybody understands. Strange, then, that she returns with the usual combination of perishables like cake and so on.

Another financial phenomenon that you are increasingly cautious towards is the "hidden extra". You are ever-vigilant for examples of this, real or imagined. Any deal, be it a business deal or merely a shopping transaction or meal out, is laden, you suspect, with hidden extras. As for holiday packages and hotel stays, you are on special guard. No little sonny Jim holiday company is going to get any hidden extras out of you in a hurry. So, out come the glasses again, onto the end of your nose they go, and you examine the small print relentlessly, to the shame of your wife and kids. But they'll be glad of it in the long run.

Everyone wants your money off you nowadays, do you

not find? As a budding Dad, you would never be so unwise or reckless as to travel anywhere by taxi. Even if you accidentally chopped all your limbs off and were in a semi-conscious state as a result (unlikely, I grant you, but stay with me) you would never even consider raising your hand and hailing a taxi. Partly because you wouldn't have a hand if you had cut your own arms off. But still, you get my point. However, even having eschewed the form of transportation known as taxis, you are still filled with horror at the prices of the alternatives. I mean, have you seen how much it costs to travel by bus nowadays? You could buy a house for that! And they're always late anyway. Couldn't run a whelk stall, that lot. So you try a train, but even for long journeys that's a rubbish idea. Just to book a train ticket over the phone you are charged a "booking fee". Pardon? A booking fee? What next, the greengrocer charging a "handling fee"? Pathetic! You could always drive but then you'll only get angry at parking fees. Not just angry – absolutely fuming!

Indeed, everywhere you look in motoring, there are things that will make you fume like a Dad. Take for example the speed camera. Just because you're no longer a boy racer, that doesn't mean you have to approve of these wretched things. They're a stealth tax and that's all there is to it. You certainly do not need anyone telling you how fast you can or cannot drive. "Good old" Jeremy Clarkson wouldn't take this lying down and neither will you, goddammit! And as for road taxes, don't get you started...

The greatest example of Dad-like tightness when it comes to motoring is with petrol. Finding the best deal for petrol becomes an important matter for a man as he gets on a bit. If he can find somewhere where it is one penny cheaper per gallon – sorry, litre – of petrol, then that garage will become his best friend, his haunt, for as long as it offers the stuff at that price. The Dad will not pause to consider whether the extra miles it takes to drive there negate the penny-per-litre saved. This will not even cross his mind. Why? Partly because he will be too busy glowing with pride at the penny saved and partly because he will be inside the petrol station, chatting away to the bored old soul behind the counter, like an Alan Partridge figure.

As we've seen elsewhere, forward planning is what turns you into your Dad. The daddy of all forward planning is found in the money-related arena. I write, of course, about the pension! Once you're turning into your Dad, you know your pension from your PEP, your ISA from your, erm, ice lolly. You are being sensible with your money, goddammit. Look after the pennies and the pounds will soon look after themselves, you keep saying. Even in your sleep. Soon, you become a real-life financial expert, brimming with wisdom on how to save the pennies.

As with all other wisdom that is accumulated as you turn into your Dad, it simply wouldn't do to keep it to yourself, would it? No, you really, really must share it as widely as possible! So make sure you become one of those pompous old bores who lectures, heckles and wags his fingers at everyone he meets. Corner people at your workplace, at parties and even in shops and tell them they're very, very silly and you're very very clever and that they really, really must listen to you. You could even chuck in the martyr line: "I'm just doing this for your own good, not mine," as you bully and hector people and wag your finger in their faces. It's not true, of course – you are doing it for your own good, so you can whip yourself into a frenzy of indignation and smugness – but they'll *never* guess that!

"You promised not to wear our investment head at this dinner party."

Indeed, even as they go cross-eyed with boredom, or even as they grab for their mobile phones to call the police and have them take you away, you don't give up. Consider yourself as someone doing them a service. As you make particularly pertinent points, make eye-contact and leave four to five seconds of dramatic silence. You are, after all, giving them a pep-talk – quite literally once you turn to Personal Equity Plans (PEPs). Once you've finished pensions and PEPs you can turn to Premium Bonds (why all the Ps, I wonder?) and repeat over and over the mantra: "And you can sell them at any time, so what have you got to lose?" Well, the interest that the money would have accumulated in a high-interest bank account for starters, but I'd hate to split hairs over it, Dad!

Perhaps the financial issue which most sharply divides the Dad and the non-Dad is that of the European single currency. You might be suspecting that the Dad is dead against the single currency, and the rest of us are for it. But it's not quite as simple as that. Instead, the real dividing line is this: the Dad has an opinion on the single currency and the rest of us don't. Not only does he have an opinion on it, he actually thinks people want to hear it. So run a mile if you ever find yourself at any form of social function and a man takes a sip of his drink and says something as ghastly as: "The whole question of the single currency is a fascinating one, don't you think?" Run, I tell you! Run like the wind!

A final financial thought for you. One of the moments of simple but profound joy as a man grows older comes when, on a Monday, you have a £20 note in your wallet. "I don't want to break into it," you think on the Tuesday when you are tempted to spend it on something frivolous. On Wednesday, too, you manage to resist the temptation to spend it. By Thursday, despite a few near-misses, it is still sitting there in all its crinkly glory. If, by Friday, you still haven't spent it, a feeling of enormous achievement shoots through your soul. It's the little things that give you a kick and this, truth be told, really is a little thing. The non-Dad would only take pride in something he has done. You, the Dad, will happily take pride in something that you have not done.

However, there is one area of money where you are little bit more gung-ho. You have been known to have the odd flutter since you began turning into your Dad. Nothing serious, just the odd lottery ticket here and there, and perhaps a wee bet on Grand National day. It's the only thing that keeps you going in life really.

So, in short: lottery tickets, yes! Eating out, no! And whatever you do, look after the pennies and let the pounds look after themselves! You're turning into your Dad, and no amount of money can hide it!

Chapter 9

Send Us A Postcard!

All this Dad-like behaviour is a lot to get used to, isn't it? New clothes to buy, a golf club to join and all that DIY – you must be exhausted! So you'll be wanting a holiday, I do believe. Here, too, your life takes on a whole new approach in your Dad years. So pack your bag, put your feet up and enjoy the holiday tour that takes you to destination Dad!

"We're only going for a week, but he's determined not to be fleeced by roadside cafes."

Talking as we were in the previous chapter about money, let's start with the financial angle of the Dad holiday first. For when you set off on holiday, you do not leave your new-found stinginess at home. Instead, it is one of the first things you pack. At literally every turn on your trip there will be an opportunity to save money. Most notably, prior to any excursion on your holiday you will be found making sandwiches to take with you. "Absolute rip-off, these tourist cafes," you say if anyone asks you what you're doing. And to be fair, you're absolutely right!

However, there are some expenses that you feel are absolutely justified on holiday and, top of the list, is the postcard. Remembering how your Dad sat you down and insisted you send postcards to your grandparents, aunties, uncles and friends, you decide it would be a lovely idea if your young family also gathered round the table and sent off notes to relatives and friends, wishing they were here and – let's be frank – boasting about what a nice time they are having and exaggerating how nice the weather is.

"But Dad," your kids might well protest, "I've been, like, texting my friends every day. So I've got nothing new to tell them." Oops! That's thrown a spanner in the works! Don't let it get in your way, though. Tell them they won't get an ice cream tomorrow unless they send at least three postcards.

So what will they write on their postcards? What thrills and spills will you all have enjoyed whilst on your trip? Or, more to the point, what exactly constitutes a summer holiday as you turn into your Dad and how does it differ from the breaks you took before you began decaying, I mean turning, into your Dad? Here's your guide... Pay attention at the back!

"On second thoughts maybe we should just text your gran and auntie."

ALL TOGETHER NOW!

The first difference you might have noticed is that you have begun to develop a dislike of anywhere hot. Or foreign. Or, to put it simply, that you need a flight or a passport to get to. So how many choices does that leave you with, when you choose where to take your next summer sojourn? Absolutely bugger all, really. So it's down to the seaside again, for you and yours! The fun – for you and, you wrongly believe, for your children – begins the moment you get into the car. You ignore their pleas for the radio to be switched on and instead try and get the whole family to join in with a jolly, jolly old chorus of sing-a-long songs.

"Why not just admit that you don't want
to holiday abroad"

"Oh I do like to be beside the seaside," you begin optimistically – and somewhat tunelessly – to be greeted only by some yawns, or perhaps an embarrassed: "Ohhh Dad!" from the back seat. Nevertheless, you soldier on with the song, convinced that if you carry on long enough and shoot enough pained expressions at your wife, she will join in, and before the second chorus comes round, your family will all be singing along like little birds.

No joy? Well, it must be that you're singing the wrong song. That'll be it, for sure. So you do another dramatic intake of breath and launch into a new song. "We're all going on a – summer holiday" you croon with exaggerated enthusiasm. Still, nobody there seems at all keen to join in with you. You feel like one of those men who try and start a chant at a football match but get it badly wrong and end up humiliated. Nobody is singing along in the car. But you carry on. Then it starts to rain. Then one of the kids starts to cry. Just like the old days, huh?

After trying to get your kids interested in a game of I-Spy (you began with a hopelessly easy one: "I spy with my little eye, something beginning with 'M'," as you drove down the, ahem, motorway) you only gave up when you realized that your kids all had iPods in their ears and that your wife had gone to sleep. No sense of fun, some people, have they? Oh well, truth be told, you could do with a little bit of peace actually. However, you break that reverie when you realize you are nearing the beach. You awaken and de-headphone the various members of your family and announce cheerily: "A shilling for the first person to see the sea!" When your Dad said this to you, you remember being extremely excited, so you cannot work out why your family is not equally gagging with ecstasy at your generous, exciting offer. Perhaps it's because they don't know what a shilling is, Dad! I mean, get with the programme, dude!

"You can stick your filthy shell. I'm listening to Arctic Monkeys."

Once at the sea, you get involved in your favourite holiday activity: walking. You walk up and down the beach, letting nothing stop you from covering the equivalent of a half-marathon. The rain, the sharp pebbles, the crapping seagulls, nothing is going to stop you. And when I say a long walk, I mean a long walk. I really do. Up hill and down dale you go, with long paces, dragging your family in your wake. They will be grateful for it in the long run, you tell yourself.

CHURCHES ARE INTERESTING

No more do you want to visit the nightclubs and bars, but you do find out where the nearest castle, abbey or similar site is. Only so recently, you would rather have died than set foot near any sort of castle or church. So what a turnaround it is to see you fiddling with your map on a windy hill, saying "It must be somewhere here" as you proceed with a field trip to the local abbey. On arrival, you will make sure your relatives come in with you and will tell them such sleep-inducing facts as: "Did you know, kids, that there has been a church on this site over for 1400 years?" How would they know that? Or: "The west end of the abbey was rebuilt in 1874 and the nave, whose walls incorporate some of the earlier church, was built in 1911." How could anyone be bored by a fact like that?

It's the same with castles. Were you generous enough to drag your little ones around Windsor Castle, you could regale them with such gems as "This was built by William the Conqueror" or even "King Edward III was born in the castle on 13 November 1312". Yes, the poor little sods will be mute with boredom within minutes of your lecture beginning but they will be pleased for it later in life. Admittedly, the drenching they get in the torrential rainstorm that marred your long walk back from the castle or abbey will not be pleasant, and therefore to argue that they will be pleased for it later in life would be stretching credibility. It will, however, most certainly be a character-building experience and therefore one that will stand them in good stead for the rest of their lives. What do you want them to be? Men or mice? (Neither, if they are female, but you get my point!)

Another favourite choice of holiday for the budding Dad is the camping holiday. Not that your family are particularly enamoured by the idea of one. When you suggest to them over dinner one day that you could all go camping this summer, you are surprised by the passion of their response. "What do you mean, no way?" you counter. Not even the prospect of barbecues every night wins them over. Imagine all the macho posturing you could have done if you had a barbecue every single night!

However, you know best so you drag them all to a camp site and your week of self-catering bliss begins. As well as the aforementioned barbecues – the Daddy of meals, as we have already seen – there is the joy of primitive dish-washing, the feeling that you are close to nature and, most importantly, the knowledge that you haven't handed over a penny of your hard-earned cash to any money-grabbing, hidden-extra hotelier who would only be ripping you off from the moment you arrived in his grubby, overrated little house to the moment you checked out.

Alternatively, you might like to consider renting a cottage on the Isle Of Wight for a week or two, as The Beatles suggested in the aforementioned *When I'm 64* on their album *Sergeant Pepper's Lonely Hearts Club Band*. Here, you have the joy of privacy and self-catering but at least, unlike camping, you do not need to worry about the inevitable rain washing you out to sea. A home from home, the cottage will be perfect for the Dad holiday. So what are you waiting for? Book one today!

"About time... my parents are keeping me here against my will."

Having had a brief break from domestic life in this chapter, it is time to return home. And as you open up your front door having been away for two weeks, the first thing you'll need to do is deal with all the post and other crap that has piled up on your doorstep in your absence...

Chapter 10

No Circulars!

Stuck to the frame of every Dad's front door is a sign which is a dead giveaway of his Dad status. "NO CIRCULARS! NO HAWKERS!" it reads. You have, after all, developed a colossal, utterly-perspective-free obsession with door-to-door salespeople and also with those "wretched sods" that put leaflets and takeaway menus through your door. You loathe them and spend much of your existence seething about the "gross, unsolicited invasion of privacy" that they commit. I mean, how dare they? It's the "Englishman's home-is-his-castle" time again, isn't it?

You simply haven't the time to go sorting your real post from these leaflets about car insurance, or takeaway menus from your local curry and pizza houses. They drive you almost as wild with rage as do the salespeople who knock on your door offering you encyclopaedias and feather dusters. There's an inherent irony here, though, if you were honest. You claim that you dislike the salespeople who knock on your door or phone you up because they waste your time. Yet, once one of these unfortunate souls appears on your doorstep or at the other end of your phone, there is no amount of time in the world that you are not willing to spend hectoring them. "I don't have time to keep answering the phone/door to you," you protest. "I'm a very busy person." As they attempt to meekly get out of your hair, you hold them there, repeating over and over and over again that you do not have time for this conversation and just wish they'd go away. You more or less ask them in for a drink while you're at it. And you trust that you'll be staying in touch!

"The 'No Circulars Notice' didn't work then?"

So it was that one Saturday morning you found yourself angrily, nay furiously, hammering the "NO CIRCULARS!" notice to your front door. This will show them, you seethed. No more will you get leaflets and pizza menus shoved through your door. Indeed, none of these people will even walk down your path. At long, long last, you will be able to relax in your own home without unwanted visitors at your door. You've struck a blow on behalf of the little guy in every neighbourhood of not just Middle England but top England and bottom England, too. Wherever they are.

So it is with disappointment and regret that you have to report that your "NO CIRCULARS" sign has been "NOT NOTICED" by anyone. You still have leaflets shoved through your door, you still have salespeople and charity workers pressing your doorbell. It seems there is no way of stopping them. However, the positive to come out of all of this is that now, when these people come anywhere near your door, you can rush to the door, rip it open and point at your sign and say: "Can't you read English?" How come you always know they are there? Surely you don't sit by your front window all day, waiting for leafleters/salespeople to appear? Ahem...

As well as sitting in your front room, waiting to give sales people what for, other activities you might like to consider as you mutate into your master include going to church and voluntary work. Let's take them in reverse order and start with the old voluntary work option. This must only be undertaken by the man who wants to retain pomposity as he turns into his Dad. You must make sure you quietly yet loudly boast about it. This can be easily pulled off by mentioning it once and then, when anyone tries to make a fuss about it, you should blush and say: "I don't want to talk about it." And it's true, you don't want to talk about it. Well not at any great length, in any case. But you want everyone to know you are doing it, don't you? It's not boasting as such, surely?

"Look out... here comes the Trumpet Voluntary."

I'LL DO MY BIT!

A favoured form of voluntary work comes in the shape of the Neighbourhood Watch group. So go and sign up and vow to "do your bit" to make this here neighbourhood a safer place. With Neighbourhood Watch you can feed your aforementioned paranoia about crime. Another reason why you don't want your holidays to take you far from home is that you are convinced that, the moment you leave home, your house will be robbed and pillaged and burnt to the ground. Literally everyone who walks down your street is, in your eyes, a robber. You've no doubt at all that the milkman only does that job because it enables him to know when people are on holiday. Likewise, when you go on holiday you refuse to get a taxi to the station or airport because you are convinced that the taxi firm monitor such bookings and dispatch people to rob the households of any family who have booked an airport drop.

So put a Neighbourhood Watch sticker on your front door and encourage, nay, hector your neighbours to do the same. Encourage them to do so with the sort of passion that will have them reaching for the phone to ring the police not because they have seen a burglary but because they are terrified by the level of harassment you have displayed since becoming the Neighbourhood Watch co-ordinator. Not that you will let any of this dissuade you from your moral crusade to bring safety and order to your local community. You're like Robert De Niro's Travis Bickle character from the film *Taxi Driver*. Only without the taxi, and – one would rather hope – the gun and psychotic rage.

But still, you can relate to his disgust at all the corruption and evil in today's society. One day a real rain will come...

"Darling, the man who robbed you blind
from the den of thieves is here."

That's why, as well as your official Neighbourhood Watch duties, you have also taken to patrolling the streets on foot, eyeing everyone you pass with a combination of suspicion and vigilance. While you are out, you might even buy a newspaper and your choice speaks volumes for what a Dad you have become.

"Blood pressures a bit high. Cut down on the *Daily Mail* and increase your broadsheet intake."

Five years ago, you barely knew the *Daily Mail* existed. Five months ago, you thought it was a pile of right-wing drivel, scaremongering about crime and asylum seekers and banging on and on about house prices. Five minutes ago you finished reading today's edition and decided it is without doubt the finest newspaper ever produced. It is quite correct about the moral decay that the country is suffering and you thought that, if anything, it under-estimated the threat we face. If you had just one criticism, it is that it might have benefited from a few more articles about house prices. But all in all, three cheers for the *Daily Mail!* Hip hip: hooray! Hip hip: hooray! Hip hip: hooray!

Praise be, indeed: which is something you might find yourself saying at the local church which you have started attending. It's not so much that you are religious – you tell people and yourself – but you like the sense of routine and the coming-together communal feel. Or, in other words, it is like your new form of nightclub but is far easier to recover from. Indeed, the communion wine you sip is hardly going to give even the Daddest of Dads a hangover.

ERM, ERM, ERM...

Now, where were we? What did you say your name was? Stuffed if I can remember! That is the sort of conversation that you will become more and more familiar with as you go down the slippery slope to becoming your father. The memory declines very sharply with age and one of the early signs of this is with people's names. There are three stages to a man's declining memory. The first is when you consistently get people's names wrong, but do so with the sort of confidence that a man with a great memory would show. Thus, you call Jake "Jack", and Will "Bill" and Jackie "Janet". You're most of the way there; indeed if you make mistakes such as these in noisy surroundings, you might even get away with it. But you have been made aware that the signs of decline are already there and you are therefore more than ready to progress to stage two of the process.

"Sorry, I'm terrible with names."

Stage two comes about directly because of your awareness of your faltering memory. Having made some "Will becomes Bill"-type errors, and having possibly been ticked off about this by your good lady wife, you approach the use of anyone's name with extreme caution. The main symptom of this is the insertion of the expression "erm, erm, erm" before you say anyone's name. It works like this: whereas before you would have said "I think you'll find, Davey", you will now say: "I think you'll find, erm, erm, erm, erm, erm Davey."

The third – and final – stage comes when you not only cease to remember what other people are called, but struggle on occasions to remember what you are called. At this point, you might as well not even bother leaving your front door and instead just remain inside, sipping lukewarm soup through a straw and rambling on about the war. Help! You're Turning Into Your Grandfather.

Chapter 11

You'll Get Square Eyes!

Have you ever found yourself, whilst watching television, suddenly getting up and switching the set off? This might seem a reasonable thing to do, and it is. *As long as you're not in company.* When the day comes that you suddenly get up and switch the set off unannounced while in company, then that's a different question all together. It's not that you were meaning to be rude, nor were you being dictatorial. You were just being a bit vague and a bit Daddish! But then everything about your television viewing habits has changed considerably of late, has it not?

I'M JUST RESTING MY EYES

Thought so! Another signpost on the road to televisual Daddom is when you increasingly fall asleep in front of the box. You might have spent the whole day looking forward to the big TV movie, even planning a special meal to eat beforehand and perhaps pouring yourself a nice glass of wine. Then, within minutes of the film starting, you find yourself thinking it would be a rather jolly idea to "rest your eyes" for a few moments. Other people watching with you might take offence at this – it is antisocial, after all. "Don't fall asleep," they'll implore you, "you've been looking forward to this all day!" You'll respond: "I'm not falling asleep, I'm just resting my eyes and listening to the television for a while."

"Could he phone you back... he's in the middle
of his favourite TV Programme."

The next thing you know, you wake up and the closing credits of the film are coming up. You've missed the whole thing, you bloody stupid idiot! Whoever was unfortunate enough to be watching the show while you snored and dribbled away will give you a knowing look that says: "Just resting your eyes, huh?" Oh well, you might reply, it's time I went up the staircase to Bedfordshire. This viewing-induced-tendency-for-coma is why you have all but stopped going to the cinema. The last time you went, you fell asleep during a film and then, as a phone rung during the on-screen action, you shouted out: "Someone answer the bloody phone" in a semi-conscious state. It was probably then that you realized you were better off doing your viewing at home, in the privacy of your own living room. (And after all, have you seen how much they charge for popcorn nowadays? HOW much?)

Admit it: you have started watching *Top Gear*, haven't you? Come on, get it off your chest. There, that feels better, doesn't it? It's better to be open about these things. Okay, so just a few years ago you couldn't have imagined liking anything involving "that old fart" Jeremy Clarkson, the right-wing buffoon! So it came as a shock to everyone – not least you – when you said, just the other day, "Talks a lot of sense does that Jeremy" after reading his column in *The Sun* while waiting to get your hair cut at the local barber's. He seems a decent young man. After all, it's not when the policemen start looking younger that you should worry, but rather it is when Jeremy Clarkson starts looking young that you know the game is up!

SSSSH! IT'S THE WINTER FORECAST

One of the biggest signposts on the road to televisual Dad-dom is when you start watching the weather forecast. No, let's be precise: it's when you start not only watching the weather forecast but actually looking forward to it and listening to it! After all, you will need to know what the weather is tomorrow so you can sensibly decide what to wear. It will pay off when you've packed an umbrella and everyone else is getting wet! You have even considered keeping a weather diary, so strong is your obsession with the weather. A weather diary! That would be something to show to the grandchildren! Not quite as interesting as war medals – but pretty damn close!

However, let's be honest: you don't study the weather just for the normal, meteorological reasons. You also watch it so you can cop a good eyeful of your favourite female weather forecaster. Every time she mentions a warm front, you feel all strange and warm yourself. Equally, when she mentions a cold snap, you imagine ways you and her could keep each other warm. You'll need a cold shower the way you are going! As for the male weather forecasters, you can greet them with a good old chorus of: "He only looks about 12! Who would fancy him? I'm sure he's wearing fake tan, the big girl's blouse!" Oh yes, it's fun, fun, fun round your place of an evening, listening to you heckle the television. They should give you your own television show, where you heckle and moan and whine about the modern world. Oh, hang on, *Grumpy Old Men* have already done that!

It's not just the weather that you are hooked on, either. You are also now in the habit of watching the news every night. It's a good habit to get into, as you keep telling anyone who does or doesn't ask you why you do it. A sombre air descends over your household at the same time each evening, you remind everyone else living there not to speak for the next 30 minutes and you sit transfixed in front of the television news. It's very strange, given how much attention you pay to the news, how little effect it seems to have on you. At the end of the news programme, you merely utter one of a small set of clichés and walk away. Among these pearls of wisdom are "Oh well, if it's not one thing it's another" or "Those politicians, they're all the same". Only the huge, huge stories seem to push you into any moment of insight or passion. Even then, it's only to say: "Well I never." Hardly up there with "I have a dream" or "The lady's not for turning," is it?

You don't just watch the news, you also flick over to *Newsnight* afterwards. And on a Friday evening, you are quite happy to tune into one of those late-night culture shows. Both are perfect for a good sleep. Indeed, if you could bottle the effect that those shows have on you, you could put valium manufacturers out of business. All it takes is a few syllables from Jeremy Paxman or Johann Hari, and you say out loud "I'm just resting my eyes for a few moments" and you're off into the land of slumber. Zzzzzzzzz. Sweet dreams, Dad!

As for daytime viewing, there are three types of programme you are increasingly getting into: documentaries,

documentaries and documentaries. Thank the lord for the advent of satellite and cable television, because now you can flick between the channels and have as much Daddy documentary viewing as you like. You can watch *Build Or Bust* on the Men & Motors channel, then skip over to Discovery for a bit of *How Do They Do It?* Hmm, what to watch next? Well you could give *SAS Desert: Are You Tough Enough?* a go on UK TV Docs or otherwise spend hour after hour watching cooking shows on UK Food. Help, your television set is turning into your Dad's one!

RADIO GA GA

Not that it's just television for you. Granted, you are probably not quite turning so much into your Dad that you have started calling the radio "the wireless" – but if you have, boy, does the title of this book really apply to you! However, as the years roll by, you have become more and more keen on your little crackly friend, haven't you? You could almost tell the whole story of your mutation into your father by tracking your listening habits. The paint stains on it, too, are Dad-like trophy stains from your DIY battles. As for what you listen to, when you moved from Radio One to Radio Two, you were turning into your Dad. When you moved from TalkSport to Five Live and then Radio Four, you were turning into your Dad. When you started listening to Classic FM in your car, the process was complete and the Dad species had bodysnatched you, never to return again.

"Do you prefer sedentary or Jurassic FM."

Five years ago, the only time you heard the voice of David Mellor discussing the merits of Beethoven and Mozart was when you were asleep and he appeared, all toothy and arrogant, during a very, very bad dream you had after unwisely consuming a colossal amount of strong Stilton cheese prior to turning in for the night. Now, you tune into classical music stations and hear him do it while you are awake! For fun! Out of your own free choice! As well as music shows, you also love a talk show, don't you? Yup, thought so. How can a week be complete without *The Archers*, *Gardeners' Question Time* or *Any Questions*? It can't, is the answer!

WHY, OH WHY, OH WHY?

However, just as huge issues fail to get much of a reaction out of you, so do trivial matters manage to turn you into a fuming, angry beast. If something gets on your nerves – and face it, what doesn't get on your nerves nowadays? – you've decided to live by the maxim: don't get mad, get even! Or, let's be precise, don't get mad, get a pen out and write an indignant letter to the local newspaper! Annoyed with inconsiderate people parking near your driveway? Get your pen out. Feel that the council could do more to take advantage of the neighbourhood's green areas? Get your pen out. Feel that young people are not showing their elders sufficient respect? Get your pen out. You don't have to live in Tunbridge Wells to be disgusted. (Though having been there, I can confirm that it probably really helps!)

"Something to sustain Sir's middle of the road rage."

As each year of your life on this here earth passes, you become more and more aware of the incompetence that dominates the world. It is almost as if as your normal eyesight fades and becomes more blurry, your ability to see incompetence sharpens. The local council? Absolute shambles. Public transport? Couldn't organize a piss-up in a brewery. Call centres? Don't get me started! The dustbin collectors? Couldn't run a whelk stall!

Then there is modern jargon. The days when you tried hard to keep up with the latest buzzwords and catchphrases are long past. No longer are you interested in blue-skying anything, nor do you care anymore whether wicked means something is awful or brilliant, or whether it just means it is wicked. As far as you are concerned, a paradigm shift is something to do with hip replacements and etiquette is something that housewives do with their curtains when they are bored. And as for pro-active, well that sounds far, far too tiring to even consider attempting. So why not write a letter to the newspaper about that, too? They might even give you your own column when they see how right you are about absolutely everything!

Once you have finished bombarding your local newspaper with fuming missives about life, the universe and everything, you can graduate to the nationals. Imagine having a letter published in *The Times*, outlining your manifesto for the world. That would show the world who's the boss! (Or, more accurately, it would show the world who's the Dad!) You might even have to accidentally leave it lying around on the table the next time your neighbours come round for another evening of you beating the living crap out of them over the *Monopoly* board! ("Oh, is that getting in your way there? It's nothing: just a letter I had published in *The Times* about how young people have no manners nowadays and how text messaging is destroying not just language but also the environment.")

DO NO PASS GO! DO NOT COLLECT £200

Which brings us to the board game. For you now, a fantastic night in involves playing cards and board games. From *Monopoly* to *Trivial Pursuit*, bridge to backgammon, you can't wait to get home from work, sit at the table and compete in these games. Compete, of course, is the operative word here. You make that Competitive Dad character from *The Fast Show* seem like some sort of left-wing nancy quitter when compared to you, who refuses to lose, you who considers anything other than a comprehensive demolition of your opponent to be an affront to your very masculinity.

However, like any primeval male of the species, to truly prove your masculinity you need to humiliate as many opponents as possible. So just demolishing the lady in your life and your close friends is not enough. Any old man could manage that. To be the alpha-male, the undisputed strutting man-hero of your neighbourhood (or, as some would see it, the tragic old fart, much giggled at on street corners as he tries to flex his muscles) you need to beat your neighbours too. So go and knock on their door, find out what are their names – nobody talks anymore nowadays, do they? I blame the television! – and demand that they come round tomorrow night for some board games. Make the demand at gunpoint if needed!

"We are neighbours officer."

With your invitations accepted, return to your house and spend the rest of the day practising your games and researching every last tip the internet has to offer on how to win each game. Then add a bit of stretching and possibly even some shadow boxing – this is serious, goddammit! When they arrive, offer a firm and to-the-point handshake. This is war, after all. Well, pretty much anyway. Make sure you beat them and then you will know that, for all your old man clothes, lack of stamina in your sporting and social life, for all your vagueness when it comes to people's names, and however much time you spend trying to save money, you can still beat that man next door at *Trivial Pursuit*.

Here we come to the end of this chapter and of the book proper. I've no doubt that you've found a lot within these pages that has made you nod sagely and say to yourself: "I know just what he means." You might have even had the odd chuckle. However, in closing, I feel a brief clarification is essential. There is nothing wrong with turning into your Dad. He is – unless your surname is West or Sutcliffe or something – probably a decent old stick and a fine example for you to follow.

Furthermore, ageing is not a process that anyone should be ashamed of, so don't be too hard on yourself or feel that anyone is laughing at you as the hair falls off and the corduroys go on. People will, in fact, be respecting your new-found paternal authority. And if you believe that, you'll believe anything!

The
Endgame

Appendix

Dad's Saturday Diary

7.15
Wakes, stretches and yawns. Realises the wife has already got up. Hmmm, she's been doing that a lot recently.

8.12
Discovers that the bathroom is occupied. Knocks on the door and tells the wife to "jolly well get a move on". (Women, huh? What do they do in there?)

8.14
Shadow-boxes while waiting for the bathroom to become free. Strains his back and, as he rubs it better, discovers to his horror how fat his lower-back is becoming.

8.30
Showers.

8.31
Leaves shower.

8.45
Takes the dog for a walk. Makes sure he keeps an eye out for any suspicious behaviour in the neighbourhood.

9.30

On returning from walking his dog, he shouts "Mind the correspondence" as he gathers up the post. None of his relatives join in with his subsequent laughter at the sheer hilarity of his catchphrase.

10.14

Walks upstairs. Forgets why he walked upstairs. Racks his brain.

10.16

Oh yes, that was it.

10.17

Dump.

10.32

Flushes and leaves toilet.

12.30

A high-fibre lunch. Well, it just makes sense doesn't it?

12.50

It's off to the DIY store to look at nails and drill attachments. HOW MUCH?! Stops off to buy a cardigan on the way home – doesn't bother trying it on in the shop. It'll fit.

14.00

A little sleep perhaps?

14.15
Has a rapturous dream about holding a barbeque party.

15.10
Wakes. Who am I?

15.30
Walks into shed, switches on the radio and moves things around for a while. He might just mow the lawn tomorrow – something to look forward to!

16.00
The wife pops her head in the shed and asks what on earth he's doing in there. Tut! Women!

16.45
The football results come in. Oh well, it's not the winning that counts, it's the taking part.

17.00
Sits down at the table with a pile of bank statements and the cheque-book stubs. Pours over them. On discovering a discrepancy gets angry, shouts at the dog and writes a letter to the local newspaper about traffic management. That'll show 'em!

17.30
Puts on slippers and feels a little calmer.

18.00
Swots up on obscure words for forthcoming game of Scrabble with the neighbours.

19.30
A nice sensible dinner with a glass of wine. Just the one, natch. Got a lawn to mow tomorrow, after all.

20.00
Watches television. Shouts at the news for a while and then closes his eyes – "just to rest them".

21.00
Woken by the wife, and it's off to bed. Night, night.

Quiz

Are You Turning Into Your Dad?

By now you should have a very good idea whether you are turning into your Dad or not. These pages have been filled with the sort of signposts that show how far down that road you are. However, if you want one final test then simply answer these questions and then refer to the Dad-o-meter at the end.

Good luck!

1. The last CD you bought was:

a) The much-hyped debut album from an up-and-coming US indie trio.

b) Brothers In Arms by Dire Straits. You already have it on vinyl in the loft but wanted a copy for your car.

c) *Top Gear* Anthems.

2. Black & Decker drills are:

a) Something your local handyman uses when he comes round to fix your door.

b) A really useful tool, you use one nearly every weekend.

c) The greatest thing that was ever invented.

3. You are given £10 and told you have one hour to spend it on whatever you want. You buy:

a) Two pints of lager and a packet of crisps and then stick the rest in the pub pool table.

b) Some petrol to put in your car. You'll be really glad of it tomorrow.

c) Five pairs of plain grey socks.

4. A good night out involves...

a) Mates, pub, alcohol, curry and nightclub and – more than likely – vomiting.

b) A sensible amount of drinking – strictly within your daily limit of alcohol units – and an early night.

c) A night out? What's that?

5. Your ideal holiday is:

a) Having it large in Ibiza. Girls, pills, beaches – lovely!

b) A fortnight in Tuscany.

c) Anywhere in England that is within driving distance of both a shingled beach and an abbey.

6. How important is it to you that your football team wins their next match?

a) Not just a matter of life or death – more important than that.

"For Heaven's sake Gerald, we all lead in the wrong suit some evenings."

b) You'd rather they won than lost but you haven't a clue who their opponents are.

c) May the best team win!

7. Neighbourhood Watch is...

a) Not sure. The name of a reality television show, maybe?

b) Those *Daily Mail* readers who do no harm but probably no good either.

c) Your new religion.

8. How important is it to you that you win next time you play bridge with your neighbours?

a) Bridge? Neighbours? Who they?

b) It'll be all right on the night, hopefully.

c) Not just a matter of life or death – more important than that.

9. Who, do you suspect, is "out to get you"?

a) Anyone and everyone during the 24 hours comedown after a heavy weekend of clubbing.

b) Possibly MI5 – they seem a little heavy-handed at times.

c) Traffic wardens probably, restaurant waiters definitely, salesmen and their "hidden extras" too.

10. Happiness is...

a) A cigar called Hamlet! Boom! Boom!

b) A nice relaxing afternoon with the missus.

c) A Sunday afternoon, simply pottering around the garden shed.

See **ratings on page 182.**

The Dad-o-Meter

If you answered mostly As: You are not turning into your Dad. You're still a groovy young lad and seem like you come from a different generation than your father. Probably because you do. Watch out, though. For you can turn into your Dad more or less overnight. Enjoy your youth while you can.

If you answered mostly Bs: You are on the way to turning into your Dad. You haven't entirely left your wild days of youth behind, but they are few and far between and leave you more tired than they used to. Expect to get pipe and slippers within a matter of years.

If you answered mostly Cs: You have turned into your Dad.

Glossary

Talking A Good Game

If you really want to turn into your Dad, you will need to learn to speak like him. So learn all these phrases and slip as many of them into conversation as you can. You might find you already use a lot of them; if so, then that really removes any doubt at all. You really are turning into your Dad.

"Answers on a postcard…"
Whenever someone asks a question, use this saying. From when you rise in the morning to when you turn in at night, always be ready to throw this one into conversation.

"As I live and breathe…"
Use this phrase to emphasize how really true your statement is. As in: "As I live and breathe, this is the most beautiful cathedral I've ever seen."

"Before you can say Jack Robinson"
To suggest something took a short amount of time. No, you won't sound clichéd.

"Break a leg"
A brilliant and witty way of wishing people luck – you'll have them rolling in the aisles!

"Cheer up, it may never happen"
One of many Dad sayings which produce the opposite effect to that intended.

"Don't mix the grain and the grape"
You'll impress everyone down your local if you keep saying this out loud.

"Eat your greens"
One of many phrases you can use at the dinner table. Others include: "carrots make you see in the dark", "spinach builds your muscles", "bread crusts make your hair curl" and, of course, "think of all those starving children in Africa". A meal is a sacred thing, after all!

"He couldn't run a whelk stall"
This is meant to be a put-down – a politer version of "He couldn't organize a piss-up in a brewery". It doesn't really work as a put-down because not being able to run a whelk stall – particularly in this day and age – wouldn't be considered the end of the world by most people. Unless they run a whelk stall, in which case they've already disproved it.

"He only looks about 12!"
When your favourite supermodel or female pop star starts dating a lithe young man, cover up your envy by saying this.

"How's that for 'mixing the grape and the grain'?"

"If this is 'just what the doctor ordered' then
I'd like to get a second opinion."

"I think you'll find..."
When you are about to disagree with someone, preface your disagreement with this. The more smug you sound, the better.

"It's not the winning, it's the taking part"
For full effect with this one, make sure you use it when somebody's team have just been beaten 7–0 by their fiercest local rivals in an ill-tempered FA Cup semi-final. And then run. Fast.

"Just what the doctor ordered!"
Only to be used at times when whatever is being discussed is not just what the doctor ordered.

"Keep your eyes peeled"
A cracker of a phrase for that day out in the car, while searching for parking spaces or for yet another antiques shop to drag your almost suicidal-with-boredom relatives round.

"Mark my words"
This is supposed to add authority and certainty to something you are about to say. Therefore, it is most used when the person is in fact consumed with doubt. Not that you're bitter.

"Natural justice will prevail"

If someone is asking for support or advice and you can't be bothered to give any, just use this cop-out phrase! Best not to give a timescale as to just when this natural justice thing will prevail.

"Neither a borrower, nor a lender be"

Or, in short, no I won't lend you 50 quid.

"Of course..."

Preface as many statements as possible with this for full, pompous Dad effect.

"Rise and shine!"

The more tired and reluctant to rise someone is, the more reason to say this. Sound as irritatingly chirpy as possible.

"Sixpence for the first person to see the sea"

So sixpence isn't part of modern currency? Who cares?

"That fits where it touches"

A mock expression of shock to use when you see somebody wearing skimpy clothing or possibly somebody looking squeezed into an item of clothing that is too small for them – usually with lascivious undertones.

" 'Natural justice will prevail' unless of course it's three points and a fine from a speed camera."

"To cut a long story short"
Something you're increasingly ill-equipped to do. Insert this sentence towards the end of a story that you've already spent around two hours recounting.

"Turn it off, you'll get square eyes"
Strangely, the only television programmes that risk giving the viewer square eyes are those television programmes you don't want to watch.

"Turn that racket off!"
Same principle as above. Your music can be played at full volume without disturbing a soul. Everybody else's music is an inconsiderate din, whatever volume it is played at.

"Waste not, want not "
A typically blithe, pithy statement. Use at as many mealtimes as possible.

"What did you say your name was?"
Self-explanatory. To come across as even more vague, get people's names slightly wrong. So Joanne becomes Joan, Beth becomes Bev and Brenda becomes Barrold.

"Where there's muck, there's brass"
Easy to say when you're no longer job-hunting and instead have your feet under the table at some jammy firm.

"Word in your shell-like"
When you want a chat with someone. To add a bit of wit to someone's life, use this during a day out at the beach. "A penny for your thoughts" is this phrase's sibling.

"You can fool some people some of the time, but you can't fool all the people all of the time"
Ideally this saying should be delivered in a tone that suggests it has never been uttered ever before. A pause in the middle adds particular theatre to the moment.

"Young people today…"
The Daddy of Daddy sayings: deliver it with as much quiet exasperation as possible.

"Young people today!"